Y0-BPU-337

St. Bernard

of

Clairvaux

(1090-1153)

by
Msgr. Leon Cristiani

Translated from the French by
M. Angeline Bouchard

ST. PAUL EDITIONS

IMPRIMATUR
✛Humberto Cardinal Medeiros
Archbishop of Boston

Original French title: **Saint Bernard de Clairvaux**

NIHIL OBSTAT
G. A. Goimard

IMPRIMATUR
J. Hottot, v.g.

ISBN 0-8198-0463-0 c
0-8198-0464-9 p

Scripture excerpts from **The New American Bible,**
copyright © 1970, used herein by permission of the
Confraternity of Christian Doctrine, copyright owner.

Library of Congress Cataloging in Publication Data

Cristiani, Leon, 1879-
    Saint Bernard of Clairvaux, 1090-1153.

    1. Bernard de Clairvaux, Saint, 1091?-1153. 2. Christian
saints — France — Clairvaux — Biography. 3. Clairvaux, France —
Biography.
BX4700.B5C6913   271'.12'024 [B]   77-4942

Copyright © 1983, by the Daughters of St. Paul

Printed in the U.S.A., by the Daughters of St. Paul
50 St. Paul's Ave., Boston, MA 02130

The Daughters of St. Paul are an international congregation of
women religious serving the Church with the communications
media.

CONTENTS

INTRODUCTION

Everyone agrees that St. Bernard was the most important man of his age, and even one of the greatest churchmen in history. He is included among the "Fathers," whose writings are the most precious Christian heritage, after the inspired writings of Scripture. He has been the subject of many biographies. The first was written by men who had witnessed at firsthand his virtues and his noble deeds — William of St. Thierry, Arnold of Bonneval, and Geoffrey of Auxerre. The first five volumes of this *Vita Prima* were examined and approved by an assembly of bishops and Cistercian abbots who gathered at Clairvaux in 1155, only two years after Bernard's death.

Besides this, St. Bernard's works, from which the liturgy has drawn many passages to be read in the Divine Office, have been published in two enormous volumes of the Migne *Patrologia Latina* (volumes 182 and 183). These are the two principal early sources.

Many works have been written about the great twelfth-century monk. One of the best known and most complete biographies is the two-volume work of Abbé Vacandard, published in Paris in 1895. As to St. Bernard's activities, one of the best documented recent works is by Watkin Williams, *Saint Bernard of Clairvaux* (Manchester, England, 1935). The great medieval scholar Etienne Gilson, of the French Academy, published a splendid study entitled *La Théologie Mystique de Saint Bernard* (Paris, Vrin, 1934). And Daniel Rops published a beautiful book entitled *Saint Bernard et ses Fils* (Tours Mame, 1962),[1] remarkable both for its text and illustrations. Why, then, another book? It will certainly add nothing to such scholarly works. It does not even address itself to historical experts, but to the general reading public who can find spiritual food and inspiration in the lives of the saints. Our purpose is to offer such readers an intimate picture of St. Bernard. This means that we shall pass rapidly over his external activities, on what might be called his public or political life. It is impossible to write about him without saying that he had a part, and sometimes the leading role, in all the important events of his century. But this little book will not seek to narrate the great events in which he was involved.

Our interest will focus especially on what went on inside of him, within his soul, in his cloistered and hidden life, his life of prayer and penance, his life of union with God and with Jesus Christ, in a word, in his religious and mystical life. After all, that is what matters most in the life of a saint. May he who now lives in divine glory, help us to understand him, to bring him to life for all who want to reconcile a deep interior life with the human condition, with earthly life which is so often insipid, tedious, and vulgar.

Bernard used to say: "God's business is mine. Nothing that concerns Him is foreign to me." We shall take this thought of his and adapt it by saying: "There is no concern of God on this earth like that of bringing saints into being." That is why nothing can be more delightful, useful, or exciting than the development of a saint. In St. Bernard we shall find a saint who is really unique in the light and love he brought to his own time and to all times, as he followed in the footsteps of his Jesus.

---

1. Translated into English by Elisabeth Abbot as *Bernard of Clairvaux, The Story of the Last of the Great Church Fathers* (New York: Hawthorn Books, Inc., 1964).

YOUTH AND THE CLOISTER

On the Road to Citeaux

During the month of April, in the year 1112, a company of young men, numbering thirty or so, set out from Châtillon-sur-Seine, in the direction of Dijon. They were traveling on foot, and carried no baggage of any sort. They had been living in community for about six months at Châtillon, devoting themselves to prayer and penance, and making unusual plans for noblemen of their time. They were going to consecrate themselves to the Lord, all at the same time, in the poorest, least known, strictest, and most austere monastery existing at that date — a monastery lost in a vast forest, and known as Citeaux.

It was a long journey from Châtillon to Citeaux. By our present-day calculations, it would be about fifty-one and a half miles to Dijon, and another twelve and a half miles to Citeaux.

It probably took our pilgrims two or three days to cover this distance. On the way, they paused — perhaps for several days — at the château of Fontaines, which was just this side of Dijon. Why did they make this stop? We shall explain that later. And who was the leader of the band? There was really no leader in the strict sense.

11

And yet among them one person stood out from the others. For six months at Châtillon-sur-Seine, he had been the animator of the group. He was not the oldest, but two of his older brothers obeyed him just like everyone else. Why? Because he had a gift, a quality that cannot be described or analyzed. He had prestige, authority, knowledge, the spirit of God, and fervor no one could resist.

His name was Bernard. Just Bernard, because family names were not yet in use. Bernard, son of Tescelin and Aleth.

But before we go any further, let us find out what these names meant. Where did Bernard come from? At the time we met him, on the road to Citeaux, he was twenty-two years old. How had he spent his outgoing youth?

The Family

We have just said that our pilgrims probably stayed for a few days at the château of Fontaines-les-Dijon. The reason for thinking so is that it was here Bernard was born in 1090. His father Tescelin and his mother Aleth both belonged to the upper nobility of Burgundy. As the vassal of the Duke of Burgundy, Tescelin was esteemed at the ducal court as a proud knight, a wise man, who understood customs and men. His outstanding virtue was loyalty, a loyalty rooted in an intense Christian faith. His wife Aleth was worthy of him. Born to the noble family of Montbard, she was the ideal lady of the manor, a refuge sent by Providence to the poor, the sick, the forsaken.

Tescelin and Aleth had seven children, six boys and a girl. Bernard was the third child. His older brothers were Guy and Gerard. After him came his sister Humbeline, and his brothers Andrew, Bartholomew, and Nivard.

For many centuries, they have been thought of as a single group of canonized saints, including the father and mother. While they have not all received the official honor of being called "Saint" or "Blessed," most of them have.

It was certainly Bernard's greatness that brought veneration to his entire family. This reminds us of another such case in the history of the Catholic Church, involving the family of St. Basil the Great in the fourth century.

Bernard's future greatness was foretold even before his birth. A delightful legend tells us how it happened. One night during Aleth's pregnancy when she may have been wondering what this child would become, she had a dream. The child appeared to her in the form of a little white dog with reddish-brown spots, who was barking ferociously. Frightened by the dream, the mother consulted a holy religious. He reportedly answered:

"The child who will be born of you will be the guardian of the house of God; he will be an excellent preacher and utterly unlike so many unfaithful dogs who cannot bark."

From that moment on, Aleth prayed harder than ever for the child she was carrying in her womb. When he was placed in her arms for the first time after his birth, she held him as high as she could toward heaven and offered him to God. She insisted on naming him Bernard, after her own father.

She was to bring up her son tenderly but with unflagging firmness. Bernard grew in devotion, simplicity, obedience, and diligence, fearless and unspoiled.

When he was old enough to go to school, the young Bernard attended the school of Châtillon-sur-Seine, which was then very famous. He soon distinguished himself by his remarkable intelligence. And so began a career in which he would always stand out and assume leadership among his peers.

A Memorable Christmas

Tescelin and Aleth had come to live in a house they owned at Châtillon, to be near their children while they were in school. In this house, probably in the year 1100 when Bernard was ten years old, an incident occurred that would greatly influence his whole life. It was the night of December 24th, Christmas Eve. The whole family was sitting by the fire, in devout preparation for Midnight Mass.

Suddenly, Bernard nodded, and was soon fast asleep. In a dream, he saw the whole Nativity scene unfold before his eyes. Jesus appeared to him, radiantly beautiful. He was able to come very close to Him and to His holy Mother. He was deep in this rapturous dream when Aleth wakened him to go to the church of Saint-Vorles with his brothers and his sister. The church bells were pealing merrily, calling the faithful to prayer.

This had apparently been just a dream. But the memory of it remained in Bernard's heart. Even when in later years he had reached the top of the mystical ladder, he liked to say that the Savior had appeared to him at the very hour of His birth one Christmas. He loved to talk about it in his sermons.

St. Francis de Sales once wrote of him: "Although, like a sacred bee, he afterwards received from all the divine mysteries the honey of a thousand sweet and divine consolations, the feast of Christmas always brought him a very special peace, and he spoke of his Master's Nativity with unparalleled delight."

This Christmas vision had a profound influence on the boy. He became "meditative," without ceasing to be a good student, a cheerful companion. He would always win love and admiration, and faithful friends were to surround him throughout his life.

But let us not imagine he was a bold, turbulent boy, always eager to thrust himself upon others and get others to imitate him. On the contrary, he was modest, in fact timid, preferring solitude and silence. He would blush like a girl when spoken to. And for all that, he exerted a quiet attraction on all who saw how gentle, pious, pure and kind he was.

We are not surprised that he had special devotion to the Virgin Mary from his earliest childhood. This devotion was to continue to grow in intensity and depth with the years, and win for him the title of *Citharista Mariae*, Mary's lute player.

First Great Bereavement

Bernard was about 16 or 17 years old when he and his family suffered their first great bereavement. Sensitive as he was, the loss of his mother Aleth left an indelible mark on him. During the summer vacation, toward the end of July in the year 1106 or 1107, Aleth announced to her family in the most matter-of-fact way that she had a premonition of her approaching death. Everyone around her protested that there was no reason to have such grim forebodings.

And yet Aleth's presentiment came true. On August 13th, the eve of the feast of St. Ambrosinian, patron of the church of Fontaines, she experienced unexpected chills and fever. With her usual vigor, the valiant chatelaine calmed everyone's fears. It was her custom to invite all the local clergy to the château to celebrate the feast. She insisted that everything should go on as planned. But this time she didn't have the strength to serve her guests with her own hands, as she always had done with charming humility.

Communion was brought to her as she lay in bed, and she received the Sacrament of the Sick. After the meal, all the guests gathered around her, to express their thanks and pay their respects. When she saw them all around her bed, she declared very quietly that she felt she was dying. They began to recite the prayers for the dying. And when they came to the invocation: "By Your passion and Your cross, deliver her, Lord," she raised her hand to make a large sign of the cross. This last effort was too much for her, and she was unable to complete the gesture. Her soul had just left her body.

Aleth's death was so simple, so calm, and yet so majestic. How could it have failed to leave an ineradicable memory in Bernard's mind? If his first biographers have given us an account of his mother's death, it is because he had told them about it. They say that Aleth appeared to Andrew, Bernard's younger brother for five years before his "conversion," that is, before he entered Citeaux with Bernard.

We cannot doubt that Bernard, even more than his brother, was haunted by the thought of his mother up to the time of his departure for monastic solitude. We know how deeply the death of his brother Gerard was to grieve him in later years. How much greater a blow, then, must his mother's death have been! It made him see the utter frailty of all earthly happiness, the beauty of faith and the splendor of eternal rewards. Aleth's death taught her son Bernard a lesson he never forgot. He learned to face every event in his life with the question: *"Quid hoc ad aeternitatem?"* – *"What does this matter for eternity?"*

The Crisis

This does not mean the problem of Bernard's vocation was now settled. He still had to choose his vocation. The "crisis" was approaching, which was to be called "the crossroads" of his life. Bernard was almost twenty. He belonged to a noble family, was endowed with a high intellect, distinguished manners, and could look forward to what the world calls "a brilliant future."

Abbé Vacandard, his most discerning biographer, has described him at this time: "His beauty, which was at once virile and gentle, attracted everyone's attention. He was of elegant stature, a little above medium height. His hair was blond, and his beard almost red. His skin was very delicate and his cheeks showed a light glow of color. His blue eyes, pure as an angel's and simple as a dove's, gave a gentle radiance to his face. His forehead bespoke grace, a grace of the spirit and not of the flesh, according to his biographer...."

But such gifts are not without peril. Bernard discovered this when he saw the frivolous and even questionable propensities of some of his noble companions. In later years he would condemn these "most unfriendly friendships" in one of his sermons. As he saw it with the eyes of a twenty-year-old youth, life in the world was a dangerous slope, and he felt himself slipping. He began to enjoy the pleasures of his worldly circle of friends. But he soon got hold of himself.

It took only two or three experiences when the demands of Christian virtue were threatened and when he came very close to the vice of impurity. His reaction was instantaneous. From the depths of his being and with the help of prayer, his spirit rose up against the flesh. To fight off the evils of a carnal temptation, he did not hesitate to jump into an icy pond and stay there until his Christian faith had overcome the demon of temptation. We are told by one of his contemporaries that it was at that moment he decided to consecrate himself totally to God in the religious life.

The Struggle

This decision was inevitably followed by a struggle. Bernard realized it would take everyone by surprise. He needed his father's consent. First, he looked around to find a reliable confidant, and found one in his uncle Gaudry, a mature man who could understand him. Gaudry did not try to dissuade him. On the contrary, he encouraged him.

It was soon apparent that something was happening to Bernard. People began to ask him questions, and he answered boldly. He had been talking with his Uncle Gaudry about the possibility of entering a cloister. This in itself was very amazing to his family. Why should a young nobleman of his status bury his talents in a monastery? But when he named the convent he had chosen, there was a general outcry. Indeed, he was talking of entering Citeaux!

Now, Citeaux was the least known, the most recently established, the strictest, the poorest, the most destitute monastery in all of Christendom. It had been founded only about twelve years earlier, in 1098, by Robert of Molesme. Life there was so poor, austere and inhuman that it was attracting practically no one at all.

The third abbot of Citeaux, Stephen Harding, continued to ask God for vocations, but still no one came. The very name of Citeaux, that pitiable convent, lost in a dark forest, made everyone quake. Bernard's brothers did everything they could to deter him from going there. They reminded him of his scholastic triumphs, of which his whole family was justifiably proud. They assured him that he had no right to bury the gifts God had generously given him.

At first, they were delighted that Bernard seemed to be yielding to their arguments. But when Bernard decided to go to a school in Germany where he could reach his full intellectual stature, he began to have doubts. As he was on his way to Germany, walking and ruminating, he came to a church. He entered

and began to pray. The thought of his mother came to
him with unbelievable force. His prayer ended in
tears. When he left the church, he turned around
and went home. He told his brothers he would go
no farther.

The Victory

All these events have brought us to the autumn
of 1111. Bernard was twenty-one. He had made up
his mind. He was going to Citeaux, and nowhere
else. But somehow he felt he should not go there
alone. Then began his victorious recruiting campaign, unique in the history of the Church. We have
already mentioned that in April, 1112, a group of
thirty or more young men were on their way to
Citeaux, to ask for admission. This was to be a kind
of rebirth for Citeaux. But how was Bernard able to
change the minds of those who were trying to retain
him in the life of the world, to the point of getting
them to renounce the world with him? Nothing like
that had ever been seen before.

In later life, Bernard was to make extraordinary
recruitments on many occasions. At his voice, monastic vocations would burgeon by the hundreds.
But his first victory was even more amazing than
those that followed.

To begin with, Bernard spoke with so much zeal
and power in revealing his intentions to his Uncle
Gaudry that the latter was the first to be conquered.
So he went with Bernard to the château of Fontaines to tell Tescelin that he wanted to enter Citeaux
with his nephew. It was like a thunderbolt. Tescelin
was a man of such strong Christian faith that he made
no objection.

But then, it seems Bernard and Gaudry cast a
ranging glance at all the young men of the family,
as though in mute invitation. Bartholomew, who was

probably sixteen to eighteen, was the first to understand. Andrew, who was a little older, hesitated. He had great love for the knightly art of arms. Bernard looked at him, and spoke to him of their mother. It was as though the presence of Blessed Aleth was palpable in the room. Andrew cried out: "I can see my mother!" Bernard answered: "That is a sign that she approves of our conversion!"

Andrew was conquered. And yet, he found it very hard to leave his brothers and his father. Turning to Bernard, he said: "Why don't you get all our brothers to give up the life of the world? If you can't do that, then divide me in half. For I cannot bear to be separated either from them or from you!"

Undaunted, Bernard continued his battle for vocations. In dealing with his eldest brother Guy, he faced obstacles of quite another sort. Guy was married and the father of two little girls, whom he loved dearly. In our own day, Bernard's project would seem utterly senseless. But let us remember that he was living at the dawn of the twelfth century, one of the great centuries of Christian faith.

Guy put up no resistance, and followed the example of his Uncle Gaudry and two of his other brothers. The only condition he set was that he obtain his wife's agreement to his plan. At first, she hesitated. But then she was taken ill, and gave the matter a second thought. She asked forgiveness for her opposition, and promised to enter a monastery herself together with her two daughters. She later became the prioress of Larrey, near Dijon. Of her daughters, one became a nun and abbess of Poulangy, while the other married Bartholomew de Sombernon.

Let us now come back to Bernard's brothers. The youngest was Nivard, but there could be no question yet of recruiting him. There was also Gerard, the second oldest son, and next before Bernard. Totally dedicated to his knightly life, Gerard at first rejected his brothers' suggestions out of hand. Bernard predicted that God would have the better of him, one way or another.

As it happened, soon afterward Gerard was wounded and taken prisoner during a siege. He then understood that the hand of God was upon him. In what is thought to be a providential manner, he managed to escape from prison. He immediately joined his brothers at Châtillon-sur-Seine. As we know, Bernard's parents owned a house there, and it was in this house that the brothers gathered to make their plans.

Throughout the land, everyone was talking about Bernard and his brothers. The name Citeaux was soon on everyone's lips. It had connotations that aroused fear, but also exerted a mysterious attraction upon the generous young knights of the area. We shall inquire later into the reasons for this astounding magnetism. One thing is certain. With each passing week, the initial group was increased with new members, until there were a total of thirty-three, of whom about thirty succeeded in carrying out their intention.

There was commotion throughout the countryside. In fact, the first biography of Bernard declared: "He became the terror of mothers and young women; friends dreaded to see him approach their friends!" Are we not justified in claiming that such a thing had never before been seen in the history of Christian monasticism?

Preparatory Retreat

It was truly a heaven-sent inspiration that led Bernard to assemble his followers at Châtillon, instead of proceeding directly to Citeaux. Without realizing it, he was offering them a kind of preliminary novitiate. He was giving them time to settle their family affairs. It is also probable that as each one joined the initital group, he provided the name of one of his friends or acquaintances who might be won over. We know that Bernard continued his recruiting campaign until the very last minute, as we shall see. In fact, he would continue until he died.

We have said that this group assembled at Châtillon-sur-Seine in the autumn of 1111. And we surmise it was in April, 1112, that the journey on foot to Citeaux began. In the interval, our young postulants were living, from all we can learn from the documents, a life of prayer and penance. As good knights of Christ, they were carrying out for Christ what was known as the "vigil of arms," *veillee d'armes* for those who were preparing for a knightly life in the world.

The day finally came when Bernard thought it was time to make a decisive move. As we know, our pilgrims stopped at Fontaines on their way. Tescelin was living there alone, with his daughter Humbeline and his youngest son Nivard. The five sons of the lord of Fontaines could not pass so close to their father's home without bidding him farewell.

Tescelin probably hid his intense feelings, and simply said to his sons, and to Bernard in particular:

"Be reasonable and moderate in all things! I know you well: it will always be hard for you to contain your zeal!"

Yes, he knew his sons very well! But he also had great love and admiration for them. He would prove it later by joining them in his turn and becoming a monk at Citeaux, where he would live out his days.

The pilgrims went to say good-bye to young Nivard, who was playing in the courtyard with some of his friends. Guy, the oldest of the brothers, thought he should say something to console him.

"See, my Nivard, we are going away! All this property will be yours! You will be very rich!"

"Indeed!" the teenager replied, as a true son of Aleth. "You are taking heaven as your portion and you leave the earth to me. I will not accept that share!"

Actually, when Nivard was sixteen, the minimum age set by the Rule, he went to Citeaux and was accepted. And so the whole family was to be there together. We shall see what was to happen to Humbeline, who would then be the only member of the family remaining in the world.

At Citeaux

At last, our thirty pilgrims arrived at Citeaux. Since January 26, 1109, the abbot of the monastery had been Stephen Harding, an Englishman and a worthy successor to Alberic and Robert of Molesme.

Abbot Stephen's prayers were answered beyond his fondest dreams. The uncertain future of his Order was now assured by the arrival of thirty new recruits, and above all of Bernard, who would lead it to unsuspected greatness.

Our young aspirants spent four days at the guest house, where they had an opportunity to affirm their intention to become monks after mature deliberation. Each of them was then received into the chapter room, in the presence of all the monks.

"What do you ask?" the abbot inquired.

"The mercy of God and yours," each of the aspirants answered in turn.

"Rise," said the abbot, for they were all prostrate before him.

The abbot then explained to them in Latin what the monastic rule would entail for them. He explained its austerities and all the demands it would make on body and soul. Then he asked each one if he felt he had the strength to carry out the Rule in its entirety.

"With the grace of God, we will do it!" was their reply.

"May God complete in you what He has begun," the abbot concluded. The entire community answered: "Amen!"

The newcomers had been accepted. They returned to the guest house for three more days. After this delay, they received the holy habit and began their novitiate.

The Novitiate

This "probation," as it was called, was to last a year. It was the hardest year of Bernard's life. During this time, he often asked himself a question that has remained famous and been repeated countless times during retreats in preparation for the religious life: "*Bernarde, ad quid venisti?*" In other words, "*Bernard, what have you come here to do?*"

The author of the first biography of Bernard has answered for him: "He entered...with the intention of dying there to the hearts and minds of men...."

Bernard used to say inwardly: "Only spirits have the right to enter here, flesh serves no purpose!"

We are fortunate in having his own explicit and trustworthy testimony on his most intimate thoughts during the early days of his monastic life.

He was guided and inspired by one thought which gave him superhuman courage, the thought of Jesus. Let us listen to his Sermon 43 on *The Song of Songs:*

"At the start of my conversion, in place of the merits I did not possess, I took care to pick a bouquet of myrrh and place it on my heart.

"I fashioned it from all the anguish and bitter sufferings of my Lord, first His sufferings as a child, then the labors and exhaustion He endured during His journeys and preaching campaigns, His vigils of prayer, His temptations in the desert, His tears of compassion, the dangers He encountered among false brothers, the insults, spittle, blows, sarcasms, ridicule, nails..., which filled His passion in such abundance.

"And among all these tiny stalks of fragrant myrrh I did not forget to place the myrrh which He was given to drink on the cross, or the myrrh used to anoint Him for His burial. As long as I live, I shall cherish the memories with which their perfume has saturated me. I shall never forget these mercies: for in them I found life....

"This sheaf of memories has been preserved for me; no one will snatch it away from me, it will remain on my breast.... In these mysteries resides the perfection of justice and the plenitude of knowledge, the riches of salvation and the treasures of merit.

"Sometimes I quaff from these mysteries a potion of salutary bitterness, and at other times I find in them the sweet oil of consolation. They sustain me in adversity and restrain me in prosperity.... That is why I so often have them on my lips, as you well know; and always in my heart, as God knows; and very often on the tip of my pen, as everyone knows. To know Jesus and Jesus crucified is the sum total of my philosophy."

The importance of the above passage cannot be overemphasized. It lays Bernard's soul bare. It is the whole Bernard, the interior Bernard, Bernard in what John of the Cross was to call "the innermost center of his soul." This is what he said to himself, and what he kept saying to everyone else. It was the secret of his power. There was to be no other until his dying day.

Bernard was completely penetrated with Christ, and Christ crucified. To fail to see this is to fail completely to understand his vocation, his life, his authority, and his prestige. Christ was his life.

In a sense, Bernard was a second St. Paul, and indeed he adopted the language and spirit of the great Apostle.

His abbot, the holy Stephen Harding, must certainly have cherished high hopes for his future in the Church. This will be clearly apparent in the next chapter.

II
CLAIRVAUX

A Founder

The sudden arrival of thirty novices at Citeaux did not pass unnoticed, in Burgundy and the neighboring provinces. A proof of this is that soon after Bernard and his band came to Citeaux, the monastery began to open other houses, and this expansion was to continue for centuries.

As our pilgrims from Châtillon-sur-Seine entered Citeaux in April, 1112, their novitiate terminated the following year, in 1113. It was on May 17, 1113, that the first daughter house of Citeaux was opened at La Ferté-sur-Grosne, in Sâone-et-Loire. A year after that, on May 31, 1114, a second foundation was made at Pontigny, which was some day to become the center for the Mission of France.

Then, in 1115, Abbot Stephen Harding formed a third team of Cistercian monks and sent them to found a monastery on the property of Count Hugo of Troyes, in the wilderness on the banks of the Aube river, at a place called "Valley of Absinthe."

And who did Stephen Harding, in his fatherly wisdom, choose to lead the group? A very young monk, only twenty-five years old, who would have twelve other monks under his orders, many of them older than he.

The young leader was Bernard of Fontaines, who would soon take the immortal name of Bernard of Clairvaux. The Valley of Absinthe would likewise soon be renamed Valley of Light — in French *"Claire Vallee,"* or more briefly, *Clairvaux.*

Under obedience, Bernard now became the founder of a monastery. While this may have surprised some of the veteran monks of Citeaux, Abbot Harding's choice would some day prove to have been divinely inspired.

Let us try to picture the solemn foundation of a new monastic order, as it was to be repeated hundreds of times during the twelfth and succeeding centuries.

The Ceremony

On the appointed day in early June, 1115, the departing monks gathered in the church of Citeaux, surrounded by the entire community. Bernard stood at the head of his group. The abbot of Citeaux, Stephen Harding, went up to the altar. Taking a crucifix, he placed it in Bernard's hands, thus appointing him abbot of the future monastery. Meanwhile, appropriate hymns were sung. Bernard left the church, armed with his cross, his companions following him in procession. Under their habits they were carrying with extreme care all the articles necessary to celebrate Mass — relics of the saints, sacred vessels, liturgical books, and priestly vestments. And without tarrying, the little band set out to the north.

Is it possible to retrace their journey? It seems that it covered a distance of some 75 miles, passing through Dijon, then probably through Messigny, Saussy, and Leuglay, until they reached the high valley of the Aube river, at Montigny-sur-Aube.

From that point, our travellers had only to follow the left bank of the Aube, going toward Bar-sur-Aube.

But about twelve and a half miles before reaching this town, and after passing through the village of Ville where one of Bernard's relatives lived, they arrived at the *"Valley of Absinthe."* Here they found a small, uninhabited vale, deep in the wilderness, but filled with sunlight on this bright June day. To the east the vale opened out onto the Aube, and a brook that ran through the little valley flowed into the river. To the west were forest-covered hills. The little enclosure measured about 3,300 to 4,000 feet in length, and was hemmed in on the north and south by ridges of roughly the same height.

It was here that Bernard decided to make a halt. He knew he was on the lands of the Count of Troyes. The exact location of the convent had evidently been left up to him. Actually, the first convent built on this site was soon too crowded, and it had to be rebuilt on a larger piece of ground close by.

The date of the foundation has been traditionally fixed as June 25, 1115.

It took the monks no more than five or six weeks to build a temporary shelter. As was the custom, they began by building the chapel, then the cemetery plot, and finally put up the wooden huts that would be their own fragile dwellings. Wood was available in abundance. Everybody set to work with enthusiasm. And although the young abbot was in rather delicate health, he gave the others the example of his own hard work.

Ordination to the Priesthood

Almost as soon as the work of building the new monastery was completed, the serious question arose of ordaining the young abbot to the priesthood. As the feast of the Assumption was approaching, Bernard understandably hoped he could be ordained before August 15th. According to Cistercian usage, the chapel of the new monastery was to be placed under the patronage of our blessed Lady. The Assumption would be the new monastery's patronal feast. It was necessary to hurry if this feast was to coincide with the abbot of Clairvaux's first Mass.

However, a difficulty arose. The new monastery was under the jurisdiction of the bishop of Langres. It was learned that this bishop had gone to attend a council at Tournus. So they had to find another prelate. They chose the bishop of Châlons-sur-Marnes, which was about 50 miles to the northwest.

The bishop of Châlons was a man of many distinctions. He was known in France and even abroad as a learned and devout man. He had been an *écolatre* or schoolman, that is to say, the superior of a school at Paris, and had founded the famous monastery of Saint-Victor, which would produce scholars of such stature as Hugo, Richard, and Adam of Saint-Victor. The name of this good bishop was William of Champeaux.

Bernard went to see Bishop William, accompanied by an older monk named Elbold. This tall and robust monk, assured and impressive in manner, completely overshadowed Bernard. In fact, the bishop greeted Elbold first, thinking he must surely be the abbot of Clairvaux. Great was his amazement to learn that the abbot was indeed this young, timid, pale and emaciated monk, standing beside Elbold.

A keen judge of men, William of Champeaux soon discerned the merit of the "servant of God" who had come to see him. He insisted on having long talks with him. And between the two men a solid friendship developed, despite the difference in their ages. In fact, it was later said of these two men: "They became as but one heart and soul in the Lord!" We can easily believe it was William of Champeaux, whose influence was great among the bishops of France, who first spread the word that Bernard was a holy, scholarly, and eloquent man. One might almost say William of Champeaux was Bernard of Clairvaux's first "godfather." He taught everyone to venerate Bernard as "an angel of God."

However, it was not until several years later that William of Champeaux's enthusiasm bore abundant fruit. One incident, we might mention, reveals how deep his friendship was for Bernard. Six years later, in 1121, when the holy bishop of Châlons saw the specter of death approaching, he decided to become a professed monk at Clairvaux and to be buried there. Such actions are far more eloquent than any words could be.

Living Arrangements

Bernard's visit to Châlons was most rewarding. We know he was ordained there, although the earliest texts tell us nothing about it. It must have been a deeply moving experience. When it was all over, Bernard returned to Clairvaux. He was needed there to supervise the construction of his monastery, and even more to provide spiritual guidance to his monks. His own way of commanding consisted above all in providing an example by his own life.

Since Bernard conceived of the monastic life as a life of penance and prayer, he took care, when he planned the living arrangements of his community, to keep for himself the poorest, the most constricted, and the least comfortable quarters. At the entrance of the dormitory, and on the same landing that communicated by a stairway with the chapel on one side and with the refectory on the other, he ordered two cells to be built. One of them was intended for distinguished guests who would visit Clairvaux. The other cell was for himself.

Let us follow one of his contemporaries into his cell. According to his account, the abbatial cell was irregular in shape. It resembled a dungeon much more than a bedroom. The curve of the stairway cut it off sharply on one side. In the very angle formed by this cutoff Bernard had placed his bed, which apparently was quite similar to the wooden crate John of the Cross would use in a later century. A block of wood, covered with straw, served as his pillow. On the other side, the cell was no more than a cupboard under the stairs. One could hardly stand erect there, and that is where the only seat was placed. The arrangement was such that whenever Bernard wanted to stand up or sit down he had to bend his head low, or he would hit the roof, which formed a thick, high wall on that side. A narrow dormer provided a little daylight. And it was there that the man whom history proclaims as the greatest figure of his time chose to live for many, many years.

We know almost nothing about the way various duties were distributed in the first monastery. It is an interesting fact, however, that the twelve companions who had left Citeaux with him to found the monastery of Clairvaux included his uncle Gaudry, and three of his brothers, Guy, Gerard, and Andrew. Gerard was appointed *cellarer*. Roughly, this means steward, the man charged with expenses and purchases. Andrew became the porter, that is, the monk who received visitors. Later when his sister Humbeline came to visit her brothers, he was the one who welcomed her.

The Years of Hardship

The monastery of Clairvaux was to become one of the most famous in the Christian world, and a Pope was to visit it in person. But that would not be until the year 1131, sixteen years later.

The first years were harder than anyone can imagine. These thirteen monks were out in the wilderness. They had no resources, and almost no help came to them from the outside. The nearest village was several miles away. They had cleared the rugged land, overgrown with scrub and thickets, which they had chosen as their new home. They had planted it as well as they could. But even in fertile soil, as this probably was, it would take many months and favorable weather conditions before any sign of crops would appear.

So at the start the monks were reduced to the most exhausting and protracted fasts. It has been said their ordinary diet consisted of coarse bread, baked from barley, millet, and vetch, ground and baked together. This bread was dark and indigestible. By way of vegetables, the monks were forced more than once to eat beech leaves, wild roots, and beechnuts. They even considered these foods a feast. We know that beechnut is an edible fruit. It resembles a triangular chestnut with a white kernel. While pigs and poultry are very fond of it, it is most unpalatable for human beings.

The abbot of Clairvaux must often have pressed on his chest that "bouquet of myrrh" of the Song of Songs that he identified with Christ's bitter sufferings on the cross.

During the summer months, the young community carried on in a spirit of peace and courage. But when winter came the supply of leaves and beechnuts was exhausted, their clothing had become threadbare through hard use. Then it seemed as though the project to found a new monastery in the wilderness was condemned by God Himself. In addition to his own exhaustion and weariness, Bernard had to face the complaints of his brothers. It did no good for him to exhort them to patience, perseverance, and trust in God. They were at the end of their strength, too. They even began to beg him to abandon such an inhospitable place.

The crisis of discouragement was at its height. All Bernard could do in his misery was to turn to God and implore His mercy. And his prayers saved the monastery. At the moment when everything seemed lost, several persons came to the monastery bringing the help they had so long awaited in vain.

In a later century, events took a similar course for John of the Cross and Teresa of Avila, when they were founding monasteries.

It is quite likely that for Bernard and his companions that first year was the hardest of all. When a harvest is slow in ripening, it rejoices everyone when it finally comes. However, there were to be other moments of hardship. St. Bernard's biographers have recorded several other crises similar to the one we have just described. But Bernard's trust never faltered.

It took about ten years before the monastery could not only feed and support its own personnel but also give the alms that were part of the rule of every convent of that era. More than once wheat bread was lacking, and had to be replaced by barley or even oat bread, bitter and indigestible.

Even when the penury of the early days gave way to prosperous times, Clairvaux remained a very penitential monastery. For a long while, milk products, fish, and eggs were never used. Even on the great feast of Easter, the menu consisted of beans and chickpeas. The cooking was always very simple. Pepper was never used, nor cumin, which was then a popular condiment. On one occasion, there was not even any salt. Bernard then called one of his monks, named Guibert.

"My son," he said to him, "take the donkey and go to the fair to buy us some salt."

"And some money?" the monk answered.

"My son, I haven't had any gold or silver for a very long time. But there is Someone above who holds all my treasures in His hands."

"Father, if I go off with nothing, I shall come back with nothing!"

"Have no fear, my son," Bernard replied, "but trust. He who has our treasures in His care will accompany you and provide you with the means of completing your errand."

Guibert set out for the fair, with serious doubts. As soon as he arrived there, he met a priest, who asked:

"Where are you from, my brother, and where are you going?"

The monk told him his story. The priest was so touched by the account that he took the monk to his house and gave him half a hogshead of salt, which was enough to load a donkey. To this he added an alm of 50 coppers which was a considerable sum in those days.

We can imagine Guibert's joy. Once back at the monastery, Bernard simply remarked:

"I told you so, and I repeat it once more. There is nothing a Christian needs so much as faith. Have faith and you will profit greatly from it all the days of your life!"

Sickness

Bernard soon had occasion to practice the ardent faith he preached to others. In fact, he had an opportunity to do so in a truly heroic manner. The various labors we have described were enough to impair the health of robust men. Now, Bernard had always been sickly. And he was so generous in offering his own actions as an example to his monks that he almost ruined his health.

It should be no surprise that he suffered most of all from a painful stomach ailment. He got so he could not digest any food at all. But he refused to spare himself by eating a less coarse diet, which would have set him apart from the other monks. In any event, more delicate food would have been very difficult to obtain. As a result, he was reduced to extreme debility.

Fortunately, his friend and protector Bishop William of Champeaux decided to visit him about this time. He found Bernard in such a piteous state that he tried to oblige him in conscience to relax some of his habitual austerities. As Bernard sternly refused in view of his duty to be an example to his community, the bishop went to Citeaux, where the general chapter was in progress. He described Bernard's condition in such terms that he was asked to do something to remedy the situation. He was also given full power to do whatever was needed.

So Bishop William returned to Clairvaux. Once there, speaking with authority in the name of the Cistercian Order, he relieved Bernard of his obligations as abbot for the duration of a year. He dispensed him from the observances of the Rule. And to make sure he would not be tempted to take part in the community life, the bishop ordered a little isolated cell to be built outside the cloister, about 450 yards from the chapel, where Bernard would not be able to hear the noise of the monastery's labors.

Once installed in his solitary cell, Bernard was put under the care of a physician who seems to have had a good reputation in the area. But the same thing happened to Bernard as was to happen to Teresa of Avila four hundred years later. The alleged physician was nothing but a charlatan. The remedies he inflicted on his patient were worse than his illness.

It was during this trying period of Bernard's life that the man who was to be his first biographer, William of St. Thierry, came to see him for the first time. This is what he has related about their meeting:

"I found him in his cell, a sort of cabin like the huts assigned to lepers at the crossroads. But I witness before God that because of the one who dwelt there, this room inspired me with as much respect as if I had been approaching the altar of the Lord. I felt penetrated with such sweet affection for the man of God, I experienced such a yearning to share his poverty, that if I had received permission, I would have attached myself to his service that very day. He welcomed us with signs of joy; and as we were inquiring about the state of his health, he said with an arch smile:

"'I feel very well, I who, until now was in command of reasonable men, by a just judgment of God am condemned to obey a brute!'"

Let us note the end of Bernard's sentence. The "brute" in question was, of course, the doctor. But Bernard obeyed him, regardless of the cost to himself.

The visitor continued:

"We ate with him, as we thought we should treat such a sick man with every consideration. But seeing that, by this doctor's orders, he was given food to eat which even a healthy, indeed a ravenously hungry person, would hardly have wanted to touch, we were most indignant. Only the rule of silence kept us from complaining aloud and pelting with insults the 'sacrilegious and homicidal' man who was thus abusing his authority. As for Bernard, that passive and resigned victim, he ate everything that was served him; everything seemed equally good to him."

Actually, Bernard had lost his sense of taste. He could no longer distinguish the tastes of various foods.

Fortunately, during Bernard's illness, the monastery continued to prosper. Perfect discipline was maintained. The monastery's fame spread, and new recruits came in ever greater numbers.

William of St. Thierry has given us a very vivid picture of the development of the monastic life at Clairvaux. He described the heroic austerities the monks practiced. But he added that Bernard's experience was not lost on him or on his followers. He had had time to meditate on what was happening to him. He had come to the conclusion that in all things, even in the rigors of penance, there was need of moderation. He realized he had gone too far and that he was leading his monks along too harsh a path. From that time on, he was to have special admiration for the virtue that he called *discretio* and that we have just called moderation. He was even inclined to esteem it, together with humility, among the very highest virtues of a monk.

Besides, in spite of the malpractice of the charlatan doctor, this year of rest was most beneficial to Bernard's health.

When the abbot resumed the active governance of his community, his first concern was to curb excesses in mortification. As some of the monks resisted what they considered a retreat from perfection, Bernard sought the help of his great friend, William of Champeaux, to arbitrate their dispute. William agreed with him, and condemned all excesses. He cited the example of the "sons of the prophets," in the days of Elijah and Elisha. Inspired by God, Elisha had mitigated the bitterness of their food, whereas the monks of Clairvaux were trying to make the unsavory food served to them even more bitter. He said to them:

"If your food has a pleasing taste, it is to God's grace that you owe it. So eat what is served to you gratefully and without qualms. To refuse to do so out of a spirit of disobedience or incredulity is to resist the Holy Spirit."

This is precisely what Bernard had discovered in his private reflections. The judgment of the renowned scholar William of Champeaux added to the young abbot's prestige. As for Bernard, he was delighted to have to restrain his monks in the ways of penance rather than reprimand their tepidity. In fact, it made him so happy that one night, between Matins and Lauds, he saw in a vision a vast throng of men of every condition coming to this blessed valley of Clairvaux to seek the secret of salvation.

In fact, during these same years — probably 1116 and 1117 — and in the years that followed, there was an extraordinary influx of new vocations at Clairvaux. It was probably in 1117 that Nivard, Bernard's youngest brother, came to take his place among his brothers. Not long afterward, their father, Tescelin, married off his only daughter Humbéline. He was left alone at Fontaines. It is thought Bernard paid him a visit in 1119 or 1120, on his way to the general chapter at Citeaux, and suggested that he join his sons. Tescelin agreed. He went to Clairvaux, and was admitted as a monk. After he had been professed and under his son Bernard's authority for about a year, he died at the monastery. The Cistercian necrology used to honor his memory on May 23.

Humbeline's Visit

Of the entire family of Fontaines, only Humbeline, the young married woman, remained in the world. Now, quite naturally, she decided to go and visit her brothers at Clairvaux. She thought she should go in her most elegant gown, as befitted a lady of her condition. She had been hearing so much good said about Clairvaux and its inhabitants that she thought she would be paying honor to Bernard and her other brothers by visiting them in her richest attire.

She was welcomed by Andrew, who was the porter. He was dumbfounded by his sister's display of luxury, and went at once to Bernard to express his amazement. Bernard in turn decided to teach his visiting sister a stern lesson. He made believe he thought she was some worldly lady or other. And he sent word to her through Andrew that he had other things to do than satisfy the idle curiosity of a woman dressed in the vain adornments of this earth. Andrew hastened to bear this message, and he rudely added:

"Why all this pomp and all these ornaments? Do they cover anything but trash?"

This was a severe rebuke. Humbeline was utterly crushed. But the blood of Tescelin and Aleth flowed in her veins, too. The memory of her mother came to her mind. She burst into tears, and cried out between her sobs:

"Yes, I am only a sinner! But it was for sinners that Christ died! It is because I am guilty that I come to seek conversation with saints. If the servant of God scorns my body, at least may my brother have pity on my soul! Let him come! Let him give orders! Whatever he commands, I am ready to do!"

When these words were relayed to Bernard, he came at once. He called his other brothers together. In a body, they came to greet their sister at the monastery door. Together, they talked about the incomparable virtues of a mother who was still very much in their thoughts.

Humbeline left Clairvaux, resolved to do honor to her family. Her husband shared her sentiments. After a few years of marriage they separated by common consent. Humbeline withdrew to the monastery of Jully-les-Nonnains. Her life as a nun merited for her the honor of being called Blessed Humbeline after her death.

The Charter of Charity

It was during the early years of Clairvaux's existence that the Cistercian *Charter of Charity* was written. Bernard was asked to participate in this task. The Cistercian Order was growing so rapidly that it needed a Constitution adapted to its new status. Abbot Stephen Harding convoked the abbots of the first four monasteries founded by Citeaux — La Ferté, Pontigny, Clairvaux, and Morimond. He wanted to join with them in preparing a rule that would be submitted to the Pope for his approval. This came to be called the *Charter of Charity*, so typical of the Cistercian spirit. It was to be confirmed by Callixtus II in a bull dated December 23, 1119, and signed at Saulieu, near Sémur in the Côte d'Or region of France.

Contrary to the situation of Cluny, where all powers were concentrated in the hands of a single abbot general, Citeaux was to have a more decentralized form of government. It was to be governed by its annual general chapters, presided over by the abbot of Citeaux. But whatever decisions were reached by these chapters would be administered by the abbots of the respective monasteries, each of whom would administer his monastery's daughter foundations. So Citeaux would have direct authority only over its daughter houses, and each of these in turn would govern the houses it had founded.

As for Citeaux, the mother house, it would be governed jointly by the abbots of her first four daughter houses. This system was quite an innovation. The monasteries were not to be totally independent of one another, as was the case in certain branches of the Benedictine Order. Nor were they all to be subject to the authority of a single man, as at Cluny. Thus, there was a wise balance between authority and independence. The original monastery asked no rents or subsidies from its daughter monasteries. Each community was to govern itself under clearly defined authority.

The proof that this was an effective system is that in less than a century the Cistercian Order had five hundred monasteries, strongly united by fraternal ties.

Cluny and Clairvaux

We shall discuss in detail the arguments that sometimes arose between the Cluniacs and the Cistercians, and in which Bernard took a very vigorous part. The foundation of Cîteaux had been in a sense a call to order addressed to Cluny.

The monastic Order of Cluny, founded in the year 910, had grown by leaps and bounds in its early years under such illustrious abbots as Berno, Odo, Aymard, Mayeul, Odilo, and Hugo.

With success had come wealth, and with wealth a certain relaxation of discipline. In a measure Cîteaux had been a protest against Cluny's tendency to laxness. Inevitably this protest created a certain ill-feeling and rivalry between the two Orders.

An early incident brought their differences to a head. A young monk, Robert of Châtillon, one of Bernard's cousins, suddenly defected from Clairvaux and placed himself under the less stringent rule of Cluny. This wounded Bernard to the heart. Robert's departure was almost like a kidnapping. His flight had been brought about by a visit to Clairvaux by the grand prior of Cluny, while Bernard was away from his monastery. Cluny, realizing its wrong, hastened to ask Rome to sanction and legitimize Robert's departure from Clairvaux.

In his sorrow, Bernard remained silent for a while. But one day he could stand it no longer and dictated one of his most eloquent letters. In this letter he apologized for his harshness, for the austerity of the Cistercian Rule. Above all, he expressed his deep regret over the loss of the one whom he called "the other half of my soul." Then he boldly took the offensive. He compared the rule of Cluny with the rule of Citeaux. And he asked: Does a soldier of Christ have the right to betray His flag, to flee from the cross?

Quite probably, Bernard's letter was intercepted by Abbot Pons, a much criticized figure who was then the abbot general of Cluny. In any event, Bernard received no answer to his letter at the time. In 1128 or thereabouts, when Peter the Venerable had succeeded Pons as abbot general, the fugitive Robert finally came to his senses and returned to Clairvaux.

In the meantime a literary debate had begun between Peter the Venerable and Bernard, born of the rivalry between the two Orders. Peter the Venerable was the first to draw his sword, countering various criticisms raised by some Cistercians against Cluny. Bernard retorted with an *Apologia* that contained certain excessively acrimonious lines. He made strong accusations against the luxurious life the monks at Cluny were leading, as well as the extravagance displayed in the splendid churches they had built, including the church of Cluny which was then at the height of its glory.

Such a debate could have had serious consequences. However, through Peter the Venerable's wise action, it had happy results. The abbot of Cluny acknowledged that while Bernard was striking hard, he was often justified in his claims. Peter the Venerable did undertake a serious reform of his Order, although not immediately. In 1132, he convoked to Cluny the great dignitaries among the "black monks," as contrasted with the "white-robed monks" of Citeaux. Two hundred priors and 1,200 brothers answered his call. And despite the resistance of some of them, statutes were written with a view to restoring the Order to the true path of holiness. Peter the Venerable spent the rest of his life seeing that they were carried out. A great friendship had sprung up between him and Bernard, to which we shall come back later.

This reconciliation between the two great Orders, which was really more complete between Bernard and Peter than among their religious, does honor to both men. It is noteworthy that Bernard, despite his youth, was already at that date the oracle of the religious life in the twelfth-century Church. Let us now try to see how Bernard understood the religious life.

III
BERNARD'S SPECIAL GIFT

A Monk

We shall soon be talking about Bernard's extensive activities outside his monastery. Here was a man, called to become the arbiter of his century, to deal with princes and kings, bishops and popes, to denounce like the ancient prophets of Israel all the abuses he discerned in Christian society. But he was first and always a monk, a monk in the fullest sense of the word.

In writing about Benedictine asceticism, Dom Berlière has said: "We cannot place too much stress on the fact that [Bernard] is not a writer wrapped up in his own individuality. He is a monk living in a community of monks, who thinks the way they do, acts as they do, and who is scrupulously faithful to the spirit of the Rule and to the daily practice of this Rule."

At Clairvaux, Bernard neglected none of his monastic duties. Untrained though he was for manual labor, he swept out the cloister, washed the refectory bowls, split logs and carried them to the wood-shed. When it was the harvest season he went out into the fields to help the lay brothers and other monks as well as he could. The only task he never performed was plowing.

His monks quickly realized how richly gifted he was in matters of the spirit. They could not remain unmoved by his eloquence. Even before entering the religious life, many of them had felt its power. It was by his fiery words that he had repulsed them when they were trying to keep him in the world. He had conquered them all, and they had followed him to Citeaux. And that was when he was only twenty-two years old!

With the years, Bernard's gifts continued to grow. His fellow monks asked him to devote himself to preaching within the monastery, instead of taking part in their manual labors, in which, for all his willingness, his failing health made him of little use. In this request, they were probably encouraged by Willam of Champeaux and by their Cistercian superiors.

In any event, that is why so many of Bernard's sermons have been preserved for posterity. He was to preach extensively, and his words were to be a moving force in the Church. He was to develop the gift of inspiring assemblies, galvanizing crowds, and setting armies in motion. But all this began very quietly within the monastery. He would one day say in a sermon, alluding to his brother-monks' thirst to hear him speak:

"I am willing to pray, to read, write, and meditate, on condition that it shall cause you no harm."

The only way Bernard could have caused his monks any harm was if he had not cooperated with God's plans for him. Obviously, these plans were to make of him the oracle of the entire Christian world. The only rival his contemporaries set up against him, and sometimes esteemed more highly, was Saint Norbert, founder of the Premonstratensians, who was a few years his senior.

But Bernard's eloquence was not merely an innate talent, a gift of nature. He had very clear-cut ideas on the apostolate that deserve to be remembered. For they belong not only to his own era but to all times, and especially to ours.

"Infusion" and "Effusion"

Bernard taught that the apostolate is a duty for those who have received from God the means of exercising it. Speaking to his monks one day, he said:

"You certainly keep for yourself what belongs to your neighbor if, having a soul overflowing with virtues and outwardly adorned with the gifts of knowledge and eloquence, you refrain, out of fear, laziness, or ill-advised humility, from uttering a good word that could be useful to others, if you keep a sterile and reprehensible silence. You deserve indeed to be called cursed, you who hide your wheat from the people instead of distributing it liberally."

But let us pay close attention! It is not permitted to devote oneself to the apostolate, relying either on grace alone or on one's talents alone. A solid and lengthy preparation is required. And this preparation consists above all in listening to God. There can be an "effusion," that is, a pouring out upon neighbor only if there is first of all an "infusion," that is, an intake of divine light into the soul.

"You dissipate and lose what is in you if, before you have completely received the *divine infusion* you hasten to pour it out.... Truly, you are depriving yourself of the life and salvation you profess to be bringing to others, when you act in this way, empty of virtues, swollen with vainglory or infected with the venom of earthly cupidity, and inwardly bloated with a moral tumor."

Thus "infusion" must precede "effusion." In other words, before activity, there must be a period of passivity. That is the time when, before speaking to others, we say with the Prophet Samuel: "Speak, Lord, for Your servant is listening!"

Bernard also said:

"Let the pond imitate the spring. The spring does not spend itself in brooks. It flows into a lake only after being quenched with its own waters. The pond need not be ashamed that its waters are not more abundant than the spring's.... First, fill your soul. Only then can you think of pouring yourself out. A benevolent and prudent charity usually superabounds, but is never exhausted."

And he concluded:

"Preach, therefore, and bear fruit, work miracles once more, outdo all wonders. There is no room left for vanity in a heart possessed by charity, for charity is the plenitude of the law and of the heart, providing it is truly total. God is charity, and nothing can fill the creature made in the image of God better than God who is charity and who alone is greater than itself."

These citations are taken from the sermon of our saint and especially from the eighty-six sermons he gave to his monks on *The Song of Songs*. We shall discuss these sermons at greater length, for they were his crowning achievement.

Bernard's Sermons

The Cistercian Rule did not provide for many formal sermons within the cloister. Actually, it required only sixteen formal sermons a year. And yet Bernard preached many more than that. This can be explained only by the monks' urgent requests for his sermons, and because, as we have said, they preferred that he spend less time in manual labor and more time in intellectual pursuits.

So, contrary to the usages of the Order, Bernard preached in every season not only on feastdays and

Sundays, but on weekdays as well. We certainly do not have the record of all his sermons. But he left us eighty-six sermons on *The Song of Songs,* and we also have eighty-six of his sermons on liturgical texts for various seasons, including four homilies on the *Praises of Mary,* seventeen homilies on the Psalm *Qui Habitat in Adjutorio Altissimi* — You Who Dwell in the Shelter of the Most High (Ps. 91). But that is not all. We have 125 of his sermons on "Various subjects," sermons on the Blessed Virgin, panegyrics of Sts. Peter and Paul, St. Andrew, St. Benedict, St. John the Baptist, and many others. Finally, we have his funeral oration for his friend St. Malachy, which we shall discuss in the proper place.

We should not think of these sermons as comparable to those ordinarily given in parish churches. Bernard used to give two sorts of sermons at the monastery. He didn't talk to the lay brothers in the same way as to the choir monks. The brothers didn't understand Latin, and so Bernard spoke to them in the dialect of the area, which was "Romansch," or if we prefer, patois. Unfortunately, no records have been preserved of these sermons.

The Latin sermons were given in the chapter room. The abbot would sit on his special chair. His monks were seated on benches along the walls. The novices were present in the place set apart for them near the professed religious. These choir monks formed an elite audience. They were all educated, reasonably advanced in the ways of the spirit. Bernard sought to develop their capacities, which he knew through their personal confidances, or intuitively sensed with the help of his own experiences.

But he intended to give all of his monks nothing less than the pure wheat of Christian doctrine. He wanted to know only Jesus Christ, and Jesus Christ crucified! This means he was continually drawing from the inexhaustible treasure of Scripture. In the

Bible he sought only Jesus, announced and pre-figured in the Old Testament, living and speaking in the New.

Concerning the Psalms, which were the principal content of the Divine Office of each day, Bernard used the charming expression: "the delightful rumination of the Psalms." He had them always in mind. He "ruminated" over them to extract their fullest savor. And what he did for the Psalms he evidently did for the whole of Scripture, so that he soon knew the entire Bible by heart. In fact, he was constantly citing passages from Scripture, almost without noticing it, just as one breathes without being aware of it.

In his Sermon 33 on *The Song of Songs*, he said: "Lord, during this mortal life, in these places of my pilgrimage, I have always had the sweet habit of grazing under Your watchful eye, and feeding on You in the Law, the Prophets, and the Psalms. Often too, I have rested in the evangelical pastures and writings of the Apostles."

The Bible was imprinted deep in his soul, like an open book, each of whose pages he knew very well.

But Bernard had also carefully studied the principal Latin Fathers, especially St. Ambrose, St. Augustine, and St. Gregory the Great, as well as St. Jerome whom he cited less. As for the Greek Fathers, he seems to have known them only through the Latin Fathers, for he referred most to Origen, who was often mentioned by St. Ambrose.

To complete this brief glimpse into the sources from which Bernard drew his knowledge, we should mention the Lives of the Desert Fathers, doubt-less according to John Cassian, as well as commentaries by Cassiodorus, the famous fifth-century author, and the "Passions" of saints like St. Andrew and St. Victor.

It should be no surprise that his knowledge of the legends of the saints was not as reliable and critical as might be wished. He was not a man to attach great value to erudition as such. He even cursed the learning that leads to scientific pride. While he did not specifically condemn the spirit of "private ownership" in knowledge and virtue, the way John of the Cross would later do, he was entirely in agreement with him with regard to the "swelling" of the ego that this spirit begets. In his Sermons on *The Song of Songs*, in which he makes so many references to himself and reveals his most secret thoughts, he sometimes says that to acquire knowledge solely for the sake of knowledge is nothing but shameful curiosity—*turpis curiositas*. And when anyone uses such knowledge to make an impression on others, that is what he calls a "shameful traffic" —*turpis quaestus*. But if one goes further and derives profit from it, that, says Bernard, is the sin of *simony* against which the great reformers of the Church of his age had so forcefully inveighed.

As for himself, Bernard wanted only to be an apostle of Christ. The only eloquence he wanted was one that scorned eloquence, and was contained in its entirety in Christ's words: "I have come to light a fire on the earth. How I wish the blaze were ignited!" (Luke 12:49)

Now, this is the fire of divine love. That is all that matters. "Woe to the knowledge that does not lead to love." This was Bernard's thought long before it was expressed by his famous compatriot, Bossuet. This is what he wanted to say in the following passage from one of his Sermons on *The Song of Songs:*

"Peter, Andrew, sons of Zebedee and the other disciples were not chosen from a school of rhetoric and philosophy; and yet it was through them that the Savior accomplished His work of salvation!" (Sermon 31, 1, on *The Song of Songs*)

In all of this, it is clear Bernard was simply obeying the Benedictine Rule which enjoined the monks to act in all things only for love of Christ, and to hold nothing dearer than Christ and the privilege of suffering with Him.

Let us listen to him again, this time in his Sermon 20 on *The Song of Songs:*

"Whoever is filled with this love [of Christ] is easily stirred with emotion by everything that relates to the Word made flesh. There is nothing he more easily listens to, nothing he reads with greater delight, nothing he meditates upon with greater serenity. Whence these holocausts of prayer that spring from the abundance of his heart. When he prays, the sacred image of the God-Man is before him. He sees Him at His birth, watches Him grow up, teach, die, rise again, ascend to heaven, and all these pictures necessarily kindle the love of virtue in his heart and calm his evil desires.

"Indeed, I am convinced that if the invisible God has willed to reveal Himself in the flesh, and to converse as a Man with men, it was in order to win first of all for His flesh the affections of carnal souls, that knew only how to love the flesh, and lead them in this way, without their realizing it, to spiritual love."

This passage clearly shows the direction Bernard wanted his monks to take. The contemplation of the mysteries of Christ's earthly life is only a sort of introduction. We must rise from "carnal" love, or *sentiment,* to *"spiritual"* love, that is to say, to the prayer of union, as the mystical writers of a later time were to call it.

Spiritual Love

We can be certain that Bernard's only ambition for his monks, as well as for himself, was to lead them to this "spiritual love." For this is the supreme goal of all holiness, of every Christian life, and therefore in a supereminent way of the monastic life, whose ideal is the very ideal of the Christian life.

To ascend a height, we must first of all have good legs. The same holds true in the spiritual order. Bernard, in his panegyric on St. Andrew, exclaimed:

"Let us ascend with the help of meditation and prayer; these will be, in a certain sense, our two feet. Meditation teaches us what we lack, and prayer obtains it for us. Meditation shows us the way, and prayer makes us advance along this way. Finally, meditation points out the dangers that threaten us, and prayer enables us to avoid them through the grace of our Lord Jesus Christ."

And whatever Bernard recommended to others, he himself practiced with great intensity. As a result, he often described the summit to which all must aim, and this summit is none other than the summit of *the love of union.*

Once again, let us turn to his Sermons on *The Song of Songs.* Here we find a passage that could have been written and spoken only by a man who had experienced it personally:

"It is of the nature of love that no one can sing its praises unless he has learned to do so by the sweetness of loving. It is not a quivering of the lips, but a hymn of the heart. It is not a sound uttered, but a movement of joy; it is a harmony of wills and not of words. It cannot be heard outwardly; it does not echo in public; no one hears it except the one who sings and the one to whom it is sung, the bride and the Bridegroom. It is a nuptial chant expressing the chaste and delightful embraces of souls, harmony of sentiment and mutuality of affection. The novice soul does not know this. To sing of love, it must have reached the perfect age, the nubile age, and have

become worthy of the Bridegroom by its virtues!"
(Sermon 1, 11, on *The Song of Songs*)

And later on, in Sermon 83, 3:

"What is more delightful than this union? What
is more desirable than this charity that unites the
soul to the Word and makes it so free that it dares
express all its desires to Him? Indeed, it is in this
that the bond of *holy marriage* consists: in the intimacy, the fusion, a fusion in which two spirits
become as one in the union of their wills, a union
elevated to the point of unity.... When God loves,
He wants only one thing: to be loved. And He loves
only so that He may be loved, knowing that love will
make all who love Him blessed. What a great thing
is love!"

We have italicized the words *holy marriage* in
the above passage. It refers, of course, to "spiritual
marriage," which all the great mystics have pointed
to as the supreme degree of love and of the mystical
life.

But everyone who reads the sermons of our
saint cannot but be inwardly warmed by their message. For in his sermons Bernard bares his soul. He
speaks of his own deepest personal experiences.
Indeed, he had no qualms in frankly admitting it
to his hearers. On one occasion, he confided:

"All night long my heart was hot within me, and
the fire burned during my meditation as I was preparing the delicacies I am about to serve you! I
speak of the fire that the Lord Jesus came to kindle
upon the earth. For, to prepare spiritual food there
must be a spiritual kitchen and a spiritual fire. Now,
I have only to distribute to you what I have prepared.
But consider the God who gives rather than the
minister who distributes. For I am only your servant
who, God knows, begs the bread of heaven and the
food of life for myself and for you. Please God, that

I may be a faithful cook and that my soul may be a useful kitchen!" (Sermon for the Feast of All Saints, 1, 2-3)

Bernard's Method

We must not compare our saint's sermons to those of the great French classical orators. Men like Bossuet and Bourdaloue, for instance, carefully organized their discourses. They would begin with a formal introduction, briefly presenting two or three clear-cut points at most, proceed to develop each of these points, and then give a peroration or conclusion. French seminarians were long taught to compose their sermons according to what might be called this obligatory method.

Bernard did nothing of the sort. In the first place, he improvised most of the time. His sermons have been preserved for us through his listeners' notes, no doubt with corrections on his part. His habitual style was what we would call the *homily*, a word that simply means "conversation" or informal talk, on a given Biblical text. Before Bernard's time, the homily had been the only method known and practiced by the great orators of the Patristic era.

Bernard followed in the footsteps of St. Augustine. Like the Bishop of Hippo, he loved to analyze words, alliterations, contrasts, verbal oppositions. Like Augustine, he was given to a certain refinement of expression, without affectation or exaggeration, however. For it is obvious that he never sought to produce an effect. What he wanted was to catch his audience, hold its attention, and make his words penetrate into the minds, indeed, the hearts of his hearers.

For example, if he wanted to preach on the nativity of Jesus, he would go about it in the simplest way possible. He would call to mind words read in the *Martyrology* in the chapter room at Prime: *Jesus Christus, Filius Dei, nascitur in Bethlehem Judae.* Jesus Christ, the Son of God, is born in Bethlehem of Judea. And he would develop each word in this sentence. He would pronounce the word *Jesus,* as though savoring all its sweetness. He discovered in it the taste of honey, a melody for the ear, a joy for the heart. And when he came to the word *nascitur,* he showed that every event in the life of Christ became a *state* that was to endure, contemporary to all ages, and passing into eternity. This inspired Bernard to exclaim that the Word is today what He was yesterday, and what He will be forever, since all the prophets, before the apostles saw Him in their own way. The Word became man, but that is as true today as it was at the time of the Incarnation. And that is why the *Martyrology* does not say: "He was born," but on the contrary: "He is born."

To conclude, Bernard would comment on the origins of the two last words: *in Bethlehem Judae.*

And then his sermon would be over. In this sermon, we have the whole of Bernard's method of preaching.

A Famous Sermon

Among Bernard's homilies on *Super Missus Est,* one has remained especially famous, and was long used in the breviary, to be read by all priests, deacons, and subdeacons. This is the sermon explaining the inner meaning of the name of Mary.

Et nomen Virginis Maria. (And the virgin's name was Mary — Luke 1:27.) This is the text on which Bernard prayerfully commented, as follows:

"The Virgin's name was Mary, which means Star of the Sea. Is this name not rightly applied to the Virgin-Mother? Is there not excellent reason to compare her to a star? Just as a heavenly body emits

its rays without suffering any lesion, so Mary brought her Child into the world without harm to her virginity. The ray comes out of the star without diminishing its brightness, and the Son is born of the Virgin without wounding her integrity.

"It is this noble star, issued from Jacob, whose light illumines the whole universe, whose splendor shines in the heavens and penetrates even into hell. She shines upon the earth, warming souls rather than bodies, reviving virtues, destroying vices. Yes, she is that brilliant and wonderful star that beneficently rules our vast sea, sparkling with merits, resplendent with virtues.

"O you who float on the tide of this world, amid storms and tempests, more than you walk on the earth, keep your eyes fixed on the star if you don't want to sink under the waves. Are you assailed by the winds of temptation, dashed against the reefs of tribulation: look up at the star, call upon Mary. Are you tossed about by the waves of pride, ambition, slander, or envy: look up at the star, call upon Mary. If anger, avarice, or the enticements of the flesh perturb the tiny skiff of your soul, look up at Mary. If you are troubled by the enormity of your crimes, ashamed by the hideousness of your conscience, terrified by the horror of your judgment, and feel you are sinking into the abyss of sadness, the whirlpool of despair: think of Mary.

"In perils, in distress, in perplexities, think of Mary, invoke Mary. Have her name always on your lips, always in your heart. And to obtain the suffrage of her prayer, be sure to follow the example of her life. As long as we follow her, we do not go astray; as long as we pray to her, we do not despair; as long as we think of her, we do not err. With her support, we cannot fall; under her protection, we fear nothing; under her guidance, we do not grow weary; with her protection, we arrive in port; and thus we experience within ourselves the truth of these words: 'The virgin's name was Mary!'"

A short comment is in order. We do not expect Bernard to offer us a scientific etymology of the name Mary. He assures us that this name signifies *Star of the Sea*. We are under no obligation to accept his view. Actually, Hebraic scholars tend to agree that the name Mary means "Lady," she who "rules," she who "commands." Certainly this meaning of the name was just as precious to him. For he loved to speak of Mary as *Notre Dame*, "Our Lady," a title that had a precise and eloquent meaning in the language of the noble knights from which he descended. So, if he had chosen to comment on this etymology of the name Mary, he would certainly have spoken in accents as eloquent as those he used in commenting on the etymology of the name Mary as Star of the Sea.

We do not look to Bernard for the science of names or words, but for the science of the heart, the science of faith and love. And this science abounds, it shines forth in all his sermons.

The Song of Songs

We should keep these remarks in mind as we come to the most brilliant series of sermons that has come down to us from Bernard, those that we have already cited: the 86 Sermons on *The Song of Songs*. Obviously, they are the product of his more mature years. The initial date of these sermons has been set around Advent, 1135. It is generally agreed that he certainly did not preach them one right after the other. Rather, he came back to this, his favorite subject, year after year, without ever finishing all he had to say about it.

The words *Song of Songs* simply mean the greatest of songs. This was one of the books of the Old

Testament. Christians accepted it from the Jews and in the same sense. There have been countless discussions on the origin of the book and on its literal meaning. It has all the earmarks of a collection of profane love songs. But the Jewish doctors had rightly discerned that profane love has the same elations, the same expressions, the same raptures, as sacred love. So they interpreted these canticles to be songs of God's love for Israel, and of Israel for its God.

Now, this love, as we have said, was like a "spiritual marriage," which Bernard conceived as the love of the soul for its God. In this, of course, he was a predecessor of Teresa of Avila and John of the Cross. With the coming of Christianity, the relations between God and Israel had become the relations between Christ and His Church. St. Paul had seen this union as the supernatural exemplar of the union between a husband and wife. Catholic commentators have always held to this interpretation. Human love is only a roughcast of true love, the love of God for us and of a human soul for its God.

Bernard was to comment on *The Song of Songs* solely in this sense. When he finally got around to it, probably in 1135, he was simply carrying out a plan he had cherished from early youth. He had been thinking about it for more than twelve years. During one of his frequent bouts with the chronic gastritis he had contracted at Clairvaux through his excessive privations, William of St. Thierry, his future biographer, came to visit him. Together, they sought to console each other amid their bodily ailments by thinking of the joys of the soul.

Their protracted conversations were in a way outlines of the sermons Bernard would later preach.

In beginning his commentary, Bernard did not ask himself any of the more or less erudite questions that modern critics formulate. He knew, as indeed we do, that this was an authentic canonical text, that is to say, it was part of divinely inspired Scripture. Therefore, this book could only be understood as dealing with true love, and there is no truer love than God's love for our souls and the love of our souls for God. In short, God is the Bridegroom, and the soul is in His presence, by His side, like a little bride who is often unfaithful, but trusting and filled with desire for God, if not with actual virtue. This thought richly nourishes devotion. So much so, that it is the norm of our relations with God, of our religious life, that is to say, of our *bond of union* with the Infinite.

Following Origen, Bernard saw *The Song of Songs* as an epithalamium, or collection of nuptial songs. It was a kind of ancient drama, involving two choirs surrounding the bridegroom and the bride, one choir being the bridegroom's friends and the other the bride's.

How are we to interpret this drama? For Bernard, there could be no doubt. The bridegroom is Jesus Christ, the God-man, who came into our midst for the express purpose of wedding the human soul. The bride is the soul or the Church, in other words, the totality of the faithful. The bride's companions are souls that are still imperfect but aspiring to perfection. Finally, the friends of the bridegroom are the angels, and saints of the Church triumphant, who protect the Church and want to see it victorious.

St. Bernard's Sermons are not a single, continuous commentary on *The Song of Songs*. He knew to whom he was speaking. His audiences were relatively mixed, in the sense that all of them had not reached the same degree of spiritual perfection. So, by turns he addressed himself to those who had advanced to great heights, and those who were lagging far behind. In speaking to the latter, he stressed the principles of Christian asceticism, purification of the soul, penance, and what is called "mortification." But he knew that after this first stage has been passed, he had to adopt a different approach. As he himself has said:

"That is a science of a very special kind; love has its own language. Anyone who does not love cannot understand it. Without a knowledge of Latin or Greek, it is not possible to understand Latin or Greek texts. The same holds true for the language of love. To anyone who does not love, the language of love will seem barbarous."

Finally, Bernard explained how he understood the language of love. We shall come back to this when we discuss the spirituality of our saint in greater detail in a later chapter.

Bernard's Popularity

From what we have just said, we can understand why Bernard's name was quickly held in honor by his contemporaries. This monk, who wanted only to be a monk, was to become a public figure, a reformer of the Church, an adversary of heretics, a counselor of kings and Popes. And he would attain this fame without seeking it, without even having wanted or aspired to it. He was always to cling to his solitude, and agree to leave it only with great reluctance. Since he was always solely concerned with doing God's will, he could not refuse to see the incontestable signs of this will in the invitations he received and the commands of his superiors.

But how did this rapid rise to fame, which we shall call his popularity, come about? How did he reach the heights of success so quickly? First we see him buried in a remote wilderness, at Clairvaux, far from all publicity. And then we see him known to everyone, sought after and admired. What caused such a change in his way of life?

The growth of Bernard's influence could probably be explained in this way. His first admirers
had been his own monks. They saw him and listened
to him every day, they were nurtured on his teaching.
They felt great gratitude toward him, and considered
it a favor from heaven to have him as a guide, teacher,
and father. They could not help telling all those with
whom they came in contact what they thought of
him. In fact, Clairvaux was experiencing a great tide
of vocations because of all the reports reaching out
in all directions.

Clairvaux came to have so many recruits that
the abbey had to establish new foundations. And
these carried afar the renown of their first abbot.
Meanwhile, William of Champeaux had spoken far
and wide about Bernard's extraordinary piety, penance, wisdom, and eloquence. Because of Bishop
William's words, other bishops, other monks outside of the Cistercian Order, wanted to see, hear,
and consult with Bernard. From one person to another, this burgeoning fame tended to grow.

Because of all this, Bernard, without even sus-
pecting it, was becoming a treasure in the Church,
a light to the Christian world, a power to be reckoned
with even by the political state, or at least by the
society of his century. And all this happened without
his even noticing it, without his ever trying to seek
his own glory from it.

Bernard did indeed leave his cloister, but with
the sole desire of returning to it as quickly as possible after completing each mission as it came up.
Each time he went out of the monastery, he thought
it was just an accident, a passing episode, a paren-
thesis that he would make every effort to close as
quickly as possible. He was a monk, and he wanted
only to remain a monk. Looking back through the
centuries, we see him as the dominant figure of his
time, to the point that any history of his century

would be incomplete without devoting a special chapter to his achievements. This is what Daniel-Rops did in his beautiful book, *L'Eglise de la Cathédrale et de la Croisade* (The Church of the Cathedrals and the Crusades). Likewise, Augustine Fliche, in Volume IX of his great History of the Church, which is entitled *Du premier Concile du Latran à l'Avènement d'Innocent III* (From the First Lateran Council to Innocent III). It is probably true, as Fliche has written, that Bernard "probably died without realizing the vital role he had played in the history of Christianity."

Fliche concludes quite rightly: "Not only did he never feel any personal ambition or court any dignity in the Church, but he always remained the contrite and humble monk who, after each mission entrusted to him, returned to recoup his energies in the solitude of the cloister and divine contemplation."

We must now watch Bernard at work, not merely in the intimacy of his monastery, but at the center of the most important affairs of the Church.

IV
BERNARD AND THE SCHISM
OF ANACLETUS

A Contested Papal Election

There is much we could say about Saint Bernard's influence outside his monastery, even before his decisive intervention in the burning question of the Schism of Anacletus. For example, we could relate the part he played in writing the Rule of the Knights Templar. But since this book is concerned principally with Bernard's inner life, we can only mention a few of the very important Church matters in which he was involved.

Perhaps the most serious of these matters came up in the year 1130. Bernard was then forty years old, and had been abbot of Clairvaux for fifteen years. He had not yet reached the height of his fame, but he was already very well known. Besides, the dangers then facing the Church were of such magnitude that he was asked to intervene, and he was the first to find some solutions to the Church's ills.

What had happened to Peter's flock?

Pope Honorius II fell ill in early February, 1130. It was soon evident that he was near death. Now, Rome was then divided into two rival clans. So profound was the cleavage that it extended even to the cardinals who had the responsibility of electing a Pope to succeed the dying Honorius II. Two families, the Frangipani and the Pierleoni were vying for power. Each of them wanted its candidate to become Pope. Among the cardinals, there was one who could see the dramatic conflict brewing. This was the Cardinal Chancellor Aimeric, titular bishop of Santa Maria Novella. He foresaw that the Pierleoni wanted to place a member of their family on the throne of St. Peter. This was Cardinal Pierleone, titular bishop of Saint Callixtus. Aimeric felt Cardinal Pierleone was unworthy of such a lofty role.

Cardinal Pierleone's greed, ambition, and weakness for simony had been denounced in a letter by the level-headed and penetrating Peter the Venerable. Another sound judge of human nature, Bishop Hubert of Lucca, in a letter to Saint Norbert, then Archbishop of Magdeburg, described Pierleone in two harsh words: *avarus et ambitiosus — covetous and ambitious.*

At all costs, Cardinal Aimeric wanted to forestall the inevitable intrigues of the Pierleone family. As Chancellor, Aimeric conceived the idea of having the dying Pope transported to the fortified monastery of Saint Gregory of Mount Coelius. There he convoked the cardinals, to take measures best suited to assure a fair papal election.

It was decided: 1) that this election would be entrusted to a commission composed of only eight cardinals, to whom the others would then give their assent; 2) that the election could not take place before Honorius II's burial; 3) that whoever opposed the first two conditions, would be excommunicated.

Then and there, the commission of eight cardinals was appointed. It included two cardinal-bishops, three cardinal-priests, and three cardinal-deacons. Pierleone was among them, as was Aimeric. In this commission, there were five partisans of the

Frangipani against three partisans of the Pierleoni. Cardinal Pierleone realized at once that his interests were in peril. He pretended the air at Saint Gregory's monastery did not agree with him, and left with his two companions.

Soon afterward, fearing he would not be correctly informed when Pope Honorius II died, Pierleone spread the rumor that the Pope was already dead, and hired a gang to attack the monastery where Honorius lay dying. The excited crowd shouted that it wanted to see the Pope if he were really still alive. The moribund Pope had to show himself at the window to put an end to the tumult. This supreme effort sapped his last remaining strength, and he died during the night of February 13th to 14th.

Chancellor Aimeric feared the riot would start all over again if he informed the three opposing cardinals of the Pope's death. He therefore decided to proceed to the election of a successor to Honorius II without them. If they were not there, he argued, it would be their own fault. So, at dawn of February 14, 1130, he hastened to bury the dead Pope quietly, in order to obey the provisions of the convention agreed to earlier. Then he went ahead and arranged for the election.

A cardinal of the Frangipani clan was elected. Cardinal Gregory di Sant'Angelo, an excellent man, was elected around eight o'clock in the morning, and the cardinals of the same clan hastened to approve the election. The newly-elected Pontiff was taken to the Lateran, where he took the name of Innocent II and received the papal insignia.

Three hours after this election, Cardinal Pierleone, who had a majority of the cardinals on his side, denounced it as failing to comply with the canonical requirements. He appealed to the people and to the clergy, and proceeded to a new election. He was the choice of his faction, and took the name of Anacletus II.

An Untenable Situation

This double election created an untenable situation. From the canonical point of view, both elections were obviously open to criticism. Granted, Innocent II had been elected first, but only by a portion of the commission charged with the election. Besides, the cardinals who later approved this election were but a minority as compared with those who had acclaimed Anacletus II. Neither faction had complied with the regulations for the election of a pontiff. These regulations had been in effect for a century, since the time of Pope Nicholas II.

According to the rules, only cardinal-bishops could participate in the election, and they were to hold a *tractatio* or discussion among themselves before proposing their choice to the other cardinals, who were priests and deacons. In this instance, there had been no *tractatio*. Unquestionably, the canonical requirements had not been fully met. On the other hand, how could a man in such disrepute as Pierleone be considered more worthy of election than his rival? It was not only doubtful, but dangerous.

So the Church had two Popes instead of one, two doubtful Popes instead of one whose election was beyond question. How could such a dilemma be solved? In the state of unrest then existing in the city of Rome, and in view of the excitement of both factions, it was impossible to reach a decision at the Sacred College to annul both elections and proceed according to all the rules.

Two solutions seemed possible: 1) to take key positions in the city of Rome; 2) to appeal to the remainder of the Church to make a choice between the two Popes who had been elected.

Pierleone understood these two solutions very well. He set in motion all of his resources in personnel and money to seize the decisive positions of the city of Rome. As early as February 15th or 16th, with the help of an army of his supporters, he drove his rival out of St. John Lateran, and took possession of St. Peter's.

Innocent II was forced to seek refuge in a fortress. He was able to resist the first assaults and to have himself consecrated in the church of Santa Maria Novella, which was the titular church of Cardinal-Chancellor Aimeric. The consecrating prelate was the cardinal-bishop of Ostia, who was legally entitled to perform the rite.

However, that same day Anacletus II also had himself consecrated. And although his consecrating prelate, Peter di Porto, did not have the privilege to perform the ceremony, it took place in St. Peter's Basilica, surely a more venerable place than the one where Innocent II had been consecrated. In any event, Innocent II no longer felt safe in Rome, and fled to the land that then wielded the greatest influence in Christendom, France.

Appeal to Christendom

Both factions immediately appealed to the Christian world. As early as February 18th, five days after his consecration, Innocent II sent Cardinal Gerard to Germany, bearing a letter for Lothair III. He notified the German king of his election as Pope, without any mention of the counter-election of Anacletus II. He further invited Lothair to come to Rome, to receive the imperial crown and "bring into submission the enemies of the Church," without designating these enemies in any greater detail.

It was a shrewd strategy. Innocent II asked no arbitration on the part of the future emperor, as this would have been contrary to the principles of the recent Gregorian reform. And Innocent II had been a strong defender of this reform, as a cardinal. But he was encouraging Lothair's hopes by promising to crown him emperor.

Anacletus II probably suspected what his rival was trying to do. So, six days later, on February 24th, he addressed a letter in his turn not only to King Lothair, but to all the bishops, all the clergy, and all the faithful of Germany. He, too, announced his election, without making the slightest mention of his rival.

Lothair therefore found himself in the most embarrassing situation. He was advised to boldly claim the right to arbitrate and completely abolish at one fell swoop all the limitations that the Gregorian Reform had placed on the emperor's powers. But he was too loyal a son of the Church to rush into such a dangerous adventure. So he gave no response to the letters he had received from the two rivals for the papal throne. Nor did he answer renewed appeals from both of them addressed to him the following May.

Three months had now elapsed without any response by Lothair to the rival Popes. It was then that France went into action. Innocent II's intuition in turning to this Christian nation had proved correct.

The Council of Etampes

What was the probable date of the Council of Etampes, which was to settle this most difficult question? We do not know. Some claim it was held in August, 1130, before Innocent II arrived on French soil. Others say it was not held until September of that year. For it is known that Innocent II, coming from Pisa and Genoa, stopped at the Monastery of Saint-Gilles about September 11th. It really doesn't matter very much. For everything moved more slowly then than now.

No document exists proving that the fugitive Pope ever asked the support of the King of France, Louis VI the Fat. One thing is certain, however. King Louis convoked a Council at Etampes, to consider the question of the double pontifical election.

The French king attended the Council, with his chief minister, Suger, abbot of Saint-Denis. It was Suger who left us an account of what happened at the Council, in his biography of the king. The archbishops of Sens, Rheims, and Bourges and their suffragan bishops were also present.

Suger declares that the king's primary concern — perhaps at Suger's suggestion — was to compare the merits of the two elected Popes and to pledge his loyalty to the more deserving of the two. Personally, Louis VI was in favor of Anacletus II, whose unfavorable aspects he did not know.

According to Suger, King Louis VI intended to discuss "more about the persons than about the election." This was wise, for it was surmised that the election had been the occasion for intrigues that could not be adequately judged.

But how was a judgment to be made regarding the two candidates for the papal tiara? Suger may have suggested it might be a good idea to send for the abbot of Clairvaux. Bernard was already having an impact on public opinion because of his great sanctity. It was thought he would be the best possible judge in a matter of this sort.

Bernard seems to have hesitated quite a while before responding to the call he had received. Who was he to become the arbiter of a conflict like this? William of St. Thierry, his first biographer and intimate friend at that time, assures us that it took a "heavenly vision" to get Bernard to make up his mind. The incident might well have occurred in this way. As always in such situations, Bernard, hesitant and trembling, sought refuge in prayer. He begged God to make His will known to him. For that was all that mattered to him. And in one form or another, he was given a sign of this divine will, which he sought in all things.

Bernard at Etampes

So Bernard set out from Clairvaux. Etampes was in the region of Rambouillet, in the region of Seine-et-Oise. It was not really a long journey, and Bernard would be called upon to make many others after the Council. His biographer has said that Bernard was received at Etampes as God's envoy. As usual, he spoke with warmth, clarity, elegance, and distinction, and of course with supernatural inspiration. And he was listened to.

On what principles did he base his judgments?

Three of his letters on the matter have been preserved. One of these, addressed to Hildebert of Lavardin, Archbishop of Tours, gives the thread of his reasoning in the clearest terms.

In agreement with the thinking of King Louis VI, Bernard attached greatest importance to the relative merits of the two candidates, from the religious and moral point of view. And in this he invoked the authority of Pope Leo the Great. This famous Pontiff had declared that in case an episcopal election were contested—and we imagine this was a frequent occurrence—the decision was to be based on the relative merits of the rivals. Bernard therefore proceeded to make such an inquiry in the case before him.

Cardinal Gregory di Sant'Angelo, who had been elected as Innocent II, had a firm reputation in the Church for his high moral standards, his piety, and his dedication to the Roman Church, and indeed for his total selflessness.

The same could not be said of his rival. Cardinal Pierleone, who had assumed the name of Anacletus II, had always been considered an ambitious man. Bernard even went so far as to say that in his youth he had been looked upon as a kind of "precursor of Anti-Christ." His private life was far from edifying. In short, a comparison between the two candidates inevitably redounded to the credit of one and the discredit of the other.

Beyond this, Bernard deemed it necessary to inquire into the mechanics of the two elections. Investigation brought out precise details on this essential point. According to Bernard, it was the *sanior pars* (the wiser portion) that declared in favor of Innocent II. By this he probably meant a majority of the cardinal-bishops, to wit, six against four. But he did not answer the possible objection that the rule demanded unanimity among the cardinal-bishops, and then a *tractatio* or discussion between them and the other cardinals. Now, there had been neither unanimity among the cardinal-bishops nor *tractatio* with the other cardinals.

Finally, Bernard's concluding argument was what he called *actio ordinabilior*, namely, that the consecration of Innocent II conformed more closely to tradition. It had been performed by the cardinal-bishop of Ostia, whereas Anacletus II had been consecrated by another prelate, contrary to the Roman custom.

We do not know exactly what transpired at the Council of Etampes. But there is little doubt that Bernard played a preponderant role in its proceedings. The fact that he was charged with writing the letters setting forth the reasons for his choice is conclusive on this point. It seems the Council agreed with his views. Louis VI, who had been in favor of

Pierleone, changed his mind and sided with the abbot of Clairvaux. He promptly sent his faithful counselor Suger to meet the new Pope who was on his way to France. The meeting took place at Cluny, and was most cordial. The Pope then continued his journey, and convened a council at Clermont on November 18, 1130, in which an anathema was pronounced against Anacletus II, in the presence of many archbishops and bishops.

Bernard in Action

Meanwhile, what had happened to Bernard? Did he just return to Clairvaux and resume his monk's life? This was surely his fondest wish. For, as we have said, he was first and above all a monk. But because of the very mystical fervor that consumed him, this man of prayer cast into the role of a man of action could not abandon the capital task he had undertaken before it was finished.

Bernard had understood the extreme peril facing the Church. In case of fire, everybody runs to the rescue. France had affirmed its loyalty. That was excellent. But didn't the remainder of the Christian world have to be won over too?

Bernard knew that the King of England, Henry Beauclerc, was on French soil, in his lands in the west, and that he hesitated to intervene. So Bernard went to see him. Where did the two men meet? We do not know precisely, but probably in the area of Chartres. At first King Henry would not agree with Bernard's arguments. He had once had dealings with Pierleone, and the English bishops were favorable to the antipope. Bernard had to refute all their objections.

As the king said he feared he would be sinning if he made the wrong choice between the two candidates for the papal crown, Bernard boldly answered him: "Worry about the other sins for which you will be answerable to God. As for this one, I take it upon myself!" This reassurance finally convinced Henry Beauclerc. He agreed to go along with France in the decision taken at the Council of Etampes. He then went to Chartres where Innocent II was staying (from January 13 to January 17, 1131), and paid him the homage of rallying to his cause. St. Bernard was present at the audience. The new Pope then asked Bernard to accompany him and eleven cardinals to the area around Liège, to obtain the loyalty of the dioceses of the north.

Germany had already decided to accept Innocent II, no doubt at the instigation of St. Norbert. Very probably, Bernard had been consulted, as the two saints were very close friends. A council had been held at Würzburg, and it had decided in favor of Innocent II. The new Pope was delighted and expressed his eagerness to meet King Lothair III of Germany. After all, only Lothair could possibly lead an expedition into Italy, if only to be crowned emperor. And it would then be up to him to drive the antipope out of Rome.

Liège was chosen as the meeting place between Innocent II and Lothair III. The German king received the Pope with great pomp, surrounded by his lords, bishops, and abbots. The meeting took place on March 22, 1131. Here again, Bernard's presence had a most important influence. It appears that Lothair, no doubt upon the advice of imprudent counselors, had intended to make certain demands upon the Pope before submitting completely to him. All we know about these demands is that Bernard referred to them in a letter as "unjust and importunate." Bernard quickly refuted the king's claims. By dint of logic and eloquence, he succeeded once more in saving the situation by avoiding the troublesome concessions Lothair demanded and defending the Pope's best interests.

Obviously, many new problems could arise, and Bernard was soon traveling over Europe and far from his monastery. The Pope needed his help to continue solving the difficulties he was constantly encountering, as Rome was still in the hands of his rival.

The Pope Visits Clairvaux

One proof of the Pope's appreciation of Bernard's services to him was his decision to visit him at his Abbey of Clairvaux before taking him along on the expedition to Italy. This expedition had been decided upon at the meeting with King Lothair at Liège, and required several months' preparation.

Innocent II returned to France, where Abbot Suger received him magnificently at Saint-Denis. Then he went to Rouen where the King of England received him. Bernard seems to have left Innocent II at Compiègne, while the Pope remained at Auxerre.

A short while later, the Pope went to visit Bernard at Clairvaux. While we are certain this visit did take place, we do not know its exact date. The historian Vacandard thinks it was probably during the summer of 1131.

Pope Innocent II was received at Clairvaux with the simplicity befitting poor monks. They went before him in a procession, holding up a wooden cross and chanting psalms in a low voice. The imposing pomp of the papal court did not distract them from their recollection. They kept their eyes downcast, repressing a curiosity that was not in line with their customs. It has been related that the Pope and cardinals were moved to tears at the sight of this monastic poverty and reserve.

The chapel of Clairvaux had been scrubbed clean. However, it was totally devoid of ornaments, sculptures, and paintings. What a contrast between the denuded style of the Cistercian churches and the magnificence of the Cluniac churches!

In the refectory, the guests of Clairvaux were received without fuss, and offered the very frugal meal the monks shared: bran bread, water to drink, cabbage as a vegetable, and to top the menu, other vegetables. No meat. At best, in honor of the occasion, a fish was served to "the Lord Pope." The other guests were allowed only to look at this delicacy. And despite this austerity, a wonderful joy pervaded the gathering. One of Bernard's earliest biographers has noted that this feast was "not an enjoyment of food, but a feast of the virtues."

During his visit to Clairvaux, the Pope developed such a close friendship with Bernard that he could no longer get along without him! And he still had great need of his services.

First, the Pope wanted Bernard at his side at the Council of Rheims, which was held in October, 1131, and during which Innocent II consecrated Louis VII the Younger as King of France.

There still remained a great uncertainty: the reconquest of Italy and Rome.

Bernard would be called on once more to intervene in this matter.

Positions of the Two Rivals at the End of 1131

Let us see why Bernard did not return to Clairvaux, at least for a prolonged stay, after the Council of Rheims. It was because of the situation existing at the end of the year 1131.

The Councils of Etampes, Würzburg, Clermont, and Rheims had assured the triumph of Innocent II.

Bernard's voice had been heeded in the lands of the Kings of France, England, and Germany, and as a consequence also in the realms of King Alphonsus VII of Castile and King Alphonsus I of Aragon. However, most of Italy and the city of Rome continued to favor Anacletus II. He, for his part, prided himself in having on his side the patriarchs of Constantinople, Antioch, and Jerusalem. Even more amazingly, Count William of Poitiers in France had adopted the cause of the antipope. In this, he was following the lead of Bishop Gerard of Angoulême, former papal legate.

Bernard was to turn his powers of persuasion to his own countrymen first.

Bernard in Aquitaine

Aquitaine, in southwestern France, was in the hands of Gerard of Angoulême. This prelate was now quite elderly, but had carried out very important missions for the Church in his youth. He was widely revered for his wisdom and clear judgment. Now, no one knows quite why but he had joined the forces of Anacletus II. And he was working on the antipope's behalf by extensive activities in the form of books, pamphlets, sermons, and propaganda campaigns in various places. Hence, the Church was in great peril in Aquitaine.

This fired Bernard with even greater zeal to come to the support of the Church and fight the schism. Some of his letters have come down to us addressed to the bishops of Aquitaine, Limoges, Poitiers, Périgueux, and Saintes, as well as to Geoffrey du Loroux, future archbishop of Bordeaux. To all he explained the reasons for his own choice and stressed the wide acceptance Innocent II already had obtained. Thus, he was able to ask the triumphant question: "Indeed, on what side is the Catholic Church?"

Bernard also refuted the claims of Gerard of Angoulême. And when he chose, he could display the talents of an irresistible polemist. We have already seen him arguing with Peter the Venerable on the monastic life. We shall later show how he had "turned Suger around," to the point of making a great friend of him. He wielded his pen with extraordinary skill.

In particular, Bernard's Letter 126, directed against Gerard of Angoulême, was a sharp satire, based on facts and proofs, seasoned with irony. In it, he showed that Gerard and his antipope had been in close contact. It was easy to see, he said, why the bishop of Angoulême sided with an antipope who had heaped favors upon him, renewed all his powers as a legate both in France and Burgundy, and extended his legation to many other countries, at least on paper. He pointed out that Gerard had first adopted the cause of Innocent II, and even written that Innocent was a saint and indeed the true Pope! But Anacletus II's advances had changed his sentiments. Bernard concluded that this demonstrated a spirit of ambition and a readiness to seek his own advantage rather than to hold fast to the truth once and for all.

Bernard's efforts were not altogether successful at the time, but they were not without results. Most of the bishops of Aquitaine adopted his views and turned against Gerard. A few years later Bernard was to return and finally bring the Count of Poitiers, Gerard of Angoulême's chief supporter, to accept the true Pope. But that would not happen until 1134 and 1135. In the meantime, we must follow our energetic abbot of Clairvaux to Italy, where he was to discover to his dismay the sad state of the city of Rome.

Bernard in Italy

We have said that the Pope "could no longer get along without Bernard." However, this does not mean that Bernard remained outside the cloister during this entire period. Not at all. He did not rejoin the Pope in Italy until 1133. In the interval, while he was very active on behalf of the true Pope, it was chiefly in his letters. He continued to devote himself to his monastic duties whenever possible.

The year 1132 was a year of intense monastic life for Bernard. And yet it was in the spring of 1132 that Innocent II left Auxere to proceed to Italy where King Lothair of Germany was to join him. The Pope and the king then set about winning the support of the cities and towns of northern Italy.

At the Pope's request, Bernard arrived in Genoa in February, 1133. His mission was to reconcile Genoa with Pisa in their conflict over the control of Corsica. Innocent II had tried to get the two cities to share control of the island. The bishoprics of Mariana, Nebbio, and Accia would be ruled by Genoa, which was to become an archbishopric. The bishoprics of Aleria, Ajaccio, and Sagone would remain suffragans of Pisa.

It was Bernard's task not only to get Genoa to accept the true Pope, but also to agree to the arrangements on Corsica. His arrival in Genoa caused a great stir in the city, which gives us some measure of his renown in the Church. Everywhere he went he was given wild ovations. He himself is our source on this.

In his Letter 129, written a year later, he said: "O what happy days! But alas! too short and too soon over! I shall never forget you, O devout people, noble nation, illustrious city! Like the prophet, I spoke out morning, noon, and night. And the eagerness of my audiences was as great as their charity.

We were bringing words of peace, and as we encountered peaceful children, our peace rested on them. How quickly this wonder was accomplished! It was as though I sowed, reaped, and loaded the sheafs of peace on my shoulders all in the same day."

The result of Bernard's efforts was the signing of a treaty of peace between Pisa and Genoa at Corneto, sometime between March 20 and March 26, 1133. This peace made Lothair's advance toward Rome much easier.

From then on, Anacletus II's star began to fade. King Roger of Naples, who had supported him, was forced to withdraw to Sicily. In Rome, the Frangipani, who had submitted to the antipope for a short time, joined with the Corsi and with Prefect Theobald to combat his authority.

Anacletus II then tried to negotiate with Lothair. He accepted him as his arbiter, hoping this would flatter him and make him transfer his loyalties to him. It looked as though the whole question as to who was the real Pope might be reopened. Bernard intervened at once with his usual forcefulness, saying: "The universal Church has spoken. It has declared itself against Anacletus and his accomplices. The case has been decided. It is not permissible to appeal in a special court a decision made by the whole of Christendom."

Lothair was convinced by Bernard's words. He marched on Rome, and entered the city on April 30, 1133, encountering no resistance. The Pisans and Genoese and some of his other allies entered the city in their turn. Innocent II was installed in the Lateran palace.

Bernard in Rome

Bernard was soon in the Eternal City, too. This was the first time he had been there. But in what a state he found it! How different the sad reality was from the pious notion of the city of Peter! Almost all the monuments bore the shocking marks of battle. The rival families had fortified their dwellings. The streets of Rome were thus lined with feudal fortresses.

The Corsi occupied the ancient temple of Jupiter Capitolinus; the Frangipani held sway on the Palatine and the Esquiline hill. The Pierleoni had taken the Transtevero as their bastion. Fortified towers rose up on every side. Beside these towers, the churches looked pitifully unimportant. All communications had been cut off between the two banks of the Tiber river, as well as between the Lateran and St. Peter's.

And what of the Roman people, living under such disastrous conditions? The city lived in an atmosphere of civil war, in a fever of hatred and rival ambitions. In his bitter disappointment, the abbot of Clairvaux developed what might be called a holy enmity against this divided city that had regressed into barbarism.

Fifteen years later, in his famous book *De Consideratione*, he said of Rome: "What shall I say about the people? It is the Roman people! I couldn't have said less and yet better expressed what I think of them!" As he saw the Romans, they were nothing but greedy and boorish men whom nothing could satisfy.

Bernard quickly realized that he did not belong in Rome. He hastened to return to Clairvaux, a long and tiresome journey in those days. Once back in his cloister, he was more disgusted than surprised to learn that Innocent II and Lothair had not been able to dislodge the Pierleone family from their positions in Rome. Lothair had to be crowned in St. John Lateran because St. Peter's was closed to him. Finally, the Germans had been driven out of Rome by the unhealthy summer air. Pope Innocent II was thus abandoned, and had to withdraw to Pisa in September, 1133.

Bernard Fights the Schism in France

When Bernard returned to France, he was still under orders to work for the cause of the true Pope. While he resumed his monastic occupations, it was not for long. He had been given full power to settle a contested election in the bishopric of Tours, where Hildebert of Lavardin had just died. He was completely successful in this difficult matter. The candidate he rejected was a deacon named Philip. After vain intrigues to become bishop, he finally yielded so completely to Bernard that he later went to Clairvaux as a penitent, and always remained a simple deacon.

Bernard was equally successful in his second journey to Aquitaine, where his great adversary had been Gerard of Angoulême. Not only had Gerard sided with the antipope, but he had usurped the see of Bordeaux in addition to his rightful see of Angoulême. Bernard soon made the suffragans of Bordeaux, the bishops of Saintes, Agen, Limoges, and Poitiers, see the evil of Gerard's ways. Soon Gerard had no one on his side but Count William of Poitiers.

Bernard realized that the time had come to use his persuasion on William. If he could separate him from Gerard, the schism was defeated in Aquitaine. So, together with Geoffrey of Chartres, Innocent II's legate, Bernard returned to Aquitaine toward the end of the year 1134.

Although Bishop Gerard advised against it, Count William consented to receive the legate and Bernard at his château of Farthenay. It was a dramatic encounter. He was at the height of his oratorical power. His words had acquired an incredible force of persuasion. And besides, he was so completely convinced of the justice of his cause! It was easy for him to make the count understand how absurd it was for a tiny region like Aquitaine to cut itself off from the universal Church.

The count declared he understood the situation, but objected that he had sworn not to allow the bishop of Poitiers to be reinstated in his see. This was a matter of feudal honor and personal loyalty. The abbot of Clairvaux then changed his arguments, and turned to more powerful means. He invited the count to attend a Mass he was going to say at the church of Notre Dame de la Couldre.

It was a memorable occasion.

The church was filled. Bernard ascended the altar steps. The bishops of Chartres and Poitiers were seated in the sanctuary.

The front of the nave was occupied by the religious, and the faithful crowded in behind them. Everyone was wondering anxiously what was going to happen. For they all knew that the count had been excommunicated as a schismatic. On this account, he had not been allowed to come beyond the threshold of the church. At the moment of Communion, Bernard suddenly turned and faced the congregation. His face seemed as if transfigured. He placed the sacred host on the paten, then everyone was dumbfounded to see him come down from the altar and walk back toward the door of the church, his eyes as though filled with lightning. When he was in front of the count, he spoke to him with great majesty:

"Well! We have begged you and you have scorned us. In our previous meeting, the multitude of God's servants assembled around you also begged you, and you did not listen. Now, behold the Son of the Virgin comes to you! He is the Head and Lord of the Church that you are persecuting. Behold your Judge, in whose name every knee bends, in heaven, on earth, and in hell. Behold your Judge, into whose hands your soul will some day fall. Are you going to rebuff Him too? Are you going to scorn Him as you have already scorned His servants?"

We can easily guess the explosive effect of this solemn reprimand. The count could not resist this totally unexpected attack. He grew faint and fell to the ground. His soldiers picked him up, but he fell down again. He looked like a dazed man. He could only utter muffled groans.

Bernard then came up to him and commanded him to rise. Then he pronounced his sentence:

"Behold before you the Bishop of Poitiers whom you drove out of his church. Go and be reconciled with him. Give him the kiss of peace and escort him personally back to his see. In obedience to God restore union and peace in your State, and pledge your loyalty to Pope Innocent, like all the rest of Christendom!"

The count was conquered, incapable of any resistance. Humbly he walked up to his bishop, gave him the kiss of peace, and escorted him back to his see, amid general rejoicing.

The whole of Aquitaine then gave up the schism. Bernard had just won one of his most amazing victories. His contemporaries were coming more and more to look upon him as a prophet. They even attributed miracles to him, and claimed he was a great miracle worker.

Bernard's Second Journey to Italy

Innocent II's fortunes were still very uncertain in Italy. The King of Sicily continued to lend all his support to the antipope. Bernard hastened to write to the people of Pisa and Genoa, to encourage them to remain faithful to the true Pope. Without going into all the details of the conflict between the Pope and the antipope in Italy, we can scarcely omit mention of Bernard's successful efforts in the city of Milan.

Milan, under the influence of its archbishop Anselm, had not pledged its allegiance to the true Pope. But Anselm had created such discontent around him because of his arrogant and domineering personality that a riot broke out against him. The unworthy prelate was besieged in his palace and forced to flee. The Council the Pope had convoked at Pisa declared he had been removed, and proclaimed his see vacant at the request of the clergy of Milan.

However, Anselm still had some followers in the city, and the Pope thought it wise to send Bernard there to restore peace and order. Here was another instance of the amazing trust everyone had in this humble monk. And once again Bernard proved that a great mystic can also be a great man of action.

Following the two cardinals who were notifying Milan of the Pope's decision at the Council of Pisa, Bernard set out in the spring of 1135. The crowd did not give its greatest acclaim to the cardinals. It was Bernard who attracted all eyes and who was received with the greatest enthusiasm. His reputation for holiness radiated like a halo around him. Everyone wanted to see him, touch his clothes, and even if possible tear off bits of his robe as relics! The sick and infirm were brought to him, as the Galileans had once done to Jesus. It was thought he could cure them with his blessing. Some even wanted to acclaim him as archbishop of Milan.

Bernard, with his usual gentleness and firmness, succeeded in freeing himself from all entreaties. He merely asked the Milanese to rally around Innocent II and King Lothair. At first, he thought he had obtained this, and went on to Pavia and Cremona where the schism was winning. But he was soon obliged to return to Milan, where Anacletus' partisans were regrouping for action.

In the end, Bernard had the last word in Milan. Its new archbishop pledged total and permanent allegiance to Pope Innocent II. Only then could Bernard return to Clairvaux and immerse himself once more in prayer and in the practice of his monastic obligations. It was in that same year, 1135, probably during Advent, that he began the magnificent series of sermons on *The Song of Songs* that he was to continue but never complete, during every free moment that would still be left to him.

To conclude our brief review of Bernard's efforts to solve the serious problem of the schism, we should note that he had to return to Italy once again in 1137 to negotiate the peace with King Roger of Sicily. He was not completely successful, but the schism soon petered out. The antipope, Anacletus II, died on January 25, 1138. His successor, Victor IV is thought to have consulted with Saint Bernard. In any event, he pledged his allegiance to Innocent II on Pentecost, May 29, 1138. The Second Lateran Council of April, 1139, wiped out the last vestiges of this painful crisis in the Church, in which Bernard had played such a prominent and constructive role.

V
BERNARD,
DOCTOR OF THE CHURCH

The Last of the Church Fathers

As we have just seen, Bernard was looked upon as a sort of prophet of the new age and as a miracle worker. He had labored for peace in the Church and won the most brilliant victories in this domain. Posterity has ratified the admiration of his contemporaries.

When we call Bernard a "Doctor of the Church," this is no mere invention on our part. This is the title officially given him by the Church. On July 17, 1830, the Sacred Congregation of Rites petitioned the Pope to raise St. Bernard to the rank of Doctor. The Pope at that time was Pius VIII, a man of great distinction who was too soon taken from his flock. In two successive decrees dated July 23, 1830 and August 20, 1830, he complied with the request of Saint Bernard's friends. It is also certain that he fulfilled the wish of the universal Church in this regard.

Long before that, two of the greatest Popes of the twelfth and thirteenth centuries, Alexander III and Innocent III, had encouraged admiration of Bernard's spiritual gifts. Since the seventeenth century, respect for Bernard has continued to grow, and Mabillon's praise of him has often been repeated: Bernard has been called the last of the Church Fathers, and in no way inferior to the others — *ultimus inter Patres, primis certe non impar.*

To understand why this is true requires a close examination of our saint's writings.

Already, in referring to him as a great Christian orator, we have touched on one of the reasons why he has been included among the Doctors of the Church. The great Doctors before him, and St. John Chrysostom in particular, had won their title by the eloquence and depth of their oratorical works. Bernard was admired by his contemporaries not only for his gift of eloquence. He was also considered to have a deep understanding of Christian doctrine.

In fact, Bernard was called upon to refute the most brilliant scholar of his time, the famous Abelard. It was around the year 1140 that Abelard began to arouse concern because of the novelty and daring of his teachings.

And yet, this was to be no easy task for Bernard, as we shall see. It will help us to understand this, if we give a quick sketch of Abelard the man.

Bernard and Abelard

Abelard was slightly older than Bernard, having been born eleven years earlier, in 1079, at Palet near Nantes. He had been given the baptismal name of Peter, and we do not know the meaning of his surname Abelard, inasmuch as his father's name was Béranger.

Peter Abelard had been the student of two famous teachers, first Roscelin, and then William of Champeaux who protected Bernard in his early days as a monk. But Abelard's original and adventurous mind was soon criticizing his teachers, and he declared himself an independent doctor. He was not more than 23 years old when he began to teach dialectics with astonishing virtuosity. First, he taught at Melun, where the French Court resided. Then he taught at Corbeil, and finally at Paris, where he opened a school of his own on Mount St. Genevieve.

Abelard soon became enamored of theology. He went to Laon to be taught this discipline by an old master of theology named Anselm, but he was not satisfied with his teacher. Upon returning to Paris, the bishop made him director of the cathedral school in 1114. He was soon known far and wide. Students came from all parts of France to study under his guidance. Among these were a future Pope, nineteen future cardinals, and fifty future bishops.

Unfortunately, in 1118 the scandal of his affair with Héloïse broke. He was obliged to withdraw from the world, retire to the monastery of Saint-Denis, and become a monk. Héloïse, meanwhile, was to become a nun. However, his reputation as a professor was so widespread that he soon resumed his teaching, first in his own monastery, then at Saint-Ayoul near Provins. Everyone agreed there was no one like him. Students flocked to him by the hundreds. And yet the question soon arose as to whether he was thoroughly orthodox, truly expounded the Church's doctrine, and was following the authentic tradition of the Church Fathers.

As early as 1121, a tract he had written, entitled *Of the Unity and Trinity of God,* was condemned by the Council of Soissons, and he was actually imprisoned for a while at Saint-Médard.

Abelard managed to get the papal legate interested in his cause, and the latter got him out of prison and back to his monastery of Saint-Denis. His audacity would soon play another trick on him. He committed the imprudence of challenging the legend of Saint Denis the Areopagite. Now, the monks were firmly convinced that Saint Denis was their original founder, and in any case a bishop of Paris and their patron saint.

Abelard's doubts were well founded, as historical research later proved. But his attack on the monastery's patron saint provoked such a storm of protest that he was forced to flee. He then built himself a peaceful oratory near Nogent-sur-Seine, which he dedicated to the Blessed Trinity. But it was soon invaded by his disciples, obliging him to build a larger convent which was to be called "The Paraclete" or "Comforter."

After various vicissitudes that would take too long to recount, Abelard returned once more to Paris and Mount Saint Genevieve which held precious memories for him. From 1136 to 1140 he continued to teach with the same success as formerly, arousing the same controversies. Was he or was he not a heretic? Some affirmed he was, others doubted it.

One of Bernard's friends, William of St. Thierry, who was to be his first biographer, wrote to him in March, 1140, to express his alarm. He had just read two of Abelard's recent works: *Introduction to Theology* and *Christian Theology*. As he saw it, Abelard was a very ambitious man who wanted to dominate Christian teaching and put his trust above all in dialectics. In fact, he had introduced dialectics into Holy Scripture, confusing matters of faith with the inventions of reason. So William of St. Thierry made the following urgent request of Bernard:

"I have turned to you, I call upon you to defend God and the whole Latin Church, because this man fears and dreads you. If you close your eyes, whom will he fear?... I assure you, your silence is a danger for you and for the Church of God...."

The Thirteen Errors

William of St. Thierry took the trouble to point out the errors he had noticed in two of Abelard's works he had just read. There were thirteen such errors. He sent them to Bernard with his own comments and refutations.

Before going any farther, let us say loudly and clearly that many people have been mistaken about Abelard in modern times. It is indeed true that he was trying to "understand" his faith, that he had a tendency to diminish the "mysteries" by dint of explaining them, and that in his mind the frontiers of faith and reason were not clearly defined. This should cause no surprise. But Abelard was nevertheless, from all we can learn about him, a believer, a devout and sincere man. In fact, he was an intensely devout man, as can be seen by the following avowal:

"I don't want to be a philosopher who contradicts St. Paul; nor an Aristotle separated from Christ."

The fact remains that he was always eagerly searching for rational explanations, and didn't always know when reason should admit its impotence and let pure faith speak out.

When Bernard read William of St. Thierry's letter, he was dismayed. Wasn't he being asked to do something beyond his capacities? He answered as follows:

"Most and almost all of these things were not known to me until now. It would be good for us to meet and discuss this matter after Easter."

So the two friends met and decided that Bernard would seek a meeting with Abelard, to confer with him and make him face up to his responsibilities, by showing him the thirteen errors that William of St.-Thierry had discovered in his recent writings.

So Bernard and Abelard met, but we don't know exactly where. Bernard began by complaining about the craze for innovations which, to his mind, were threatening the Church's doctrine. Abelard agreed with him. But then the abbot of Clairvaux tried to make him understand that he, Abelard, was an "innovator," indeed, that he dealt in his writings with the Trinity, the Incarnation, the Redemption, and original sin in too human a way, and that his very method was dangerous. This Abelard refused to concede.

And yet Bernard was right on that occasion. Abelard's intentions were good. But his language was vague, intemperate, ambiguous, in a word, dangerous for orthodoxy.

Too often, Abelard played with words, thinking he was explaining something that was really beyond explanation, and apparently succeeding only in confusing the minds of his readers. In the matter of sin in particular, Abelard ended up with pure Pelagianism, without realizing it. His explanations of the Blessed Trinity were akin to Sabellianism. He was not intentionally a heretic. But his manner of speaking often "smelled of heresy," to use the language of the time.

Abelard's way of explaining the relationship between reason and faith could lead to serious misunderstanding. On the one hand, he was eager to prove that reason was powerless to penetrate the Infinite that is God. But on the other hand, he affirmed over and over again that *nothing can be believed unless it is first understood.*" This led him to consider faith as an opinion, and not as a firm and irrevocable adherence founded on God's sovereign authority. He seemed unable to discern between adherence founded on God's authority and acceptance based on human reason. Clarity was not one of the marks of his definitions.

Let us see what Bernard found to condemn in Abelard's thinking in general. In the treatise he finally published on Abelard's errors, he declared in no uncertain terms, and perhaps with some exaggeration:

"This man argues about faith against faith. He sees nothing as an enigma, nothing in a mirror, but looks at everything face to face. Of all that exists in heaven and on earth, he deigns to ignore nothing, unless it be himself. He changes the limitations set by our Fathers when they discussed the loftiest questions of Revelation. In teaching his disciples, who are still novices, immature, scarcely weaned from dialectics, scarcely able to understand the primary elements of faith, he throws open the mystery of the Trinity, that is to say, the Holy of Holies and the King's chamber."

While Abelard admitted that the mysteries of faith are above reason, he had a tendency to compare the philosophers to the inspired prophets. As a result, according to the historian Vacandard, he ended up with "a sort of mystical rationalism that claimed to be Christian."

The Council of Sens

Bernard's discussions with Abelard had produced no tangible results. Bernard tried to warn the public, especially students, against Abelard's books and teachings. Soon the only subject of conversation in educated circles was the quarrel between these two men, equally famous but for different reasons.

As usual, there was a difference of opinion. Abelard, egged on by his more fanatical disciples, was hardening his positions. Among these disciples was a dangerous figure, Arnold of Brescia, who would soon be talked about in the most vexatious way. Although Abelard had promised Bernard he would revise his doctrines and retract those that would be proved false, he now decided to defend himself. He requested a public confrontation with the abbot of Clairvaux before a council of bishops.

This is precisely what Bernard wanted to avoid out of a spirit of charity and humility. Abelard must have thought—or his friends and disciples may have advised him—that in view of his superior practice in "dialectics" he could easily defeat a monk who was certainly considered holy, but not initiated in the dialectical methods of the schools.

As it happened, there was soon to be a large gathering of bishops at the cathedral of Sens on the first Sunday after Pentecost, on the occasion of an exposition of the relics of certain saints. The King of France would be there, for at that time Sens was the ecclesiastical metropolis to which Paris, then only a bishopric, was attached.

Abelard therefore wrote to the Archbishop of Sens proposing that he transform the gathering into a true council, where he could defend his opinions against those who attacked them. He had not mentioned Bernard by name. But everyone knew that he was Abelard's adversary. So the Archbishop hastened to transmit Abelard's letter to Bernard, adding that he had granted Abelard's request.

Bernard, taken by surprise by this new approach, at first refused to attend the council. He pleaded his incompetence, his lack of practice in dialectical debate, his desire not to "let divine reason be agitated by paltry human reasons." Besides, he pointed out that Abelard's writings were there for anyone to read. It was up to the bishops to judge them, and not his responsibility.

However, there was so much talk about the prospective encounter that Bernard found he could not refuse to join battle with Abelard without danger to Christian truth. Once he decided to act, not without some regrets, he set about preparing for the debate.

In particular, he prepared the arguments he would need at the coming Council of Sens.

To begin with, Bernard wrote to the bishops, advising them that they were to come to Sens not as simple spectators but as judges. Then, he reviewed with the greatest care the propositions — that is to say, the thirteen errors — which William of St. Thierry had declared suspect in Abelard's writings. On the eve of the debate, June 2, 1140, he held a preliminary conference with the bishops, during which he produced Abelard's writings, and read certain passages that he deemed dangerous. He demonstrated their lack of orthodoxy, using proofs from Scripture and Tradition, especially Saint Augustine.

The bishops were convinced. Now, they needed only to listen to Abelard and pronounce their verdict.

The first session was held on June 3rd in the cathedral church of Saint Stephen. Abelard appeared to be very confident. He was sure he had an answer ready for everything that the Council would say. We shall soon see what his answer would be.

The abbot of Clairvaux was invited to speak first, in his capacity of "defender of the faith." He refused from the start to take part in any debate, but limited himself to setting forth the erroneous propositions. Now, he had not thirteen, but seventeen such propositions taken not only from Abelard's two works, *Introduction to Theology* and *Christian Theology,* but also from two others: *Know Yourself,* and the *Book of Sentences.* Then Bernard called upon the author either to repudiate his own texts or correct the errors they contained, or else justify them by theological arguments.

It was a magnificent opportunity for Master Abelard, who was so sure of his ability to defend his ideas. To the stupefaction of all present Abelard simply announced that he challenged the Council and would appeal to the Pope. He had been told the

Curia admired his works and talent, and that Rome would side with him against his adversaries. The members of the Council urged him to change his mind, but to no avail.

It is quite possible that Abelard had learned about the private meeting on the previous evening. He may have thought the bishops had been stirred up against him in advance, and were determined to condemn him no matter what he said. In this connection, we might point out that among Abelard's students was a young Roman, the subdeacon Hyacinth, who would be elected fifty years later as Pope Celestine III. Perhaps young Hyacinth suggested that Rome would judge him more favorably than the French bishops.

Abelard's response at first threw the Council into turmoil. But after all, it was Abelard who had requested to appear before the Council. He could not now withdraw his request. Rome would have its say, no one could object to that. But the Council would first have to pass judgment on the matter. That was Bernard's view. Hyacinth's efforts to frighten the bishops by threatening them with Rome's displeasure had no effect. It made no difference to the bishops that Hyacinth was well-thought-of in Rome and belonged to the powerful Orsini family.

The trial followed its course in the following manner. Instead of condemning Abelard in person, the judges reread the seventeen propositions Bernard had submitted. Those that might be given an orthodox interpretation were set aside. Only fourteen that were judged unacceptable were retained and formally condemned.

Abelard's Defeat

We have no record of subdeacon Hyacinth's argument. But one of Bernard's letters indicates that he had cast doubt among the bishops. What would

Rome say? This is what the bishops kept asking them-selves. On this occasion, Bernard displayed rare prudence and skill. Pope Innocent II certainly knew him well, for Bernard had rendered valuable service to him in times past.

The abbot of Clairvaux therefore wrote three very pressing letters to the Pope, two of them in the name of the archbishops of Sens and Rheims and their suffragans, the third in his own name. In these letters he set forth all the facts, giving the reasons for Abel-ard's condemnation. He recalled the excitement this quarrel had caused in the schools and even among the faithful, and begged the Holy See to pass a decisive sentence. The synodal letter, which Bernard had composed, concludes:

"If Your Holiness deigned to impose silence upon Master Peter, forbidding him to teach and to write, and suppressed his books strewn with per-verse dogmas, you would be pulling thorns and brambles out of the sanctuary; and the harvest of Christ would still have the strength to grow, to flower, and produce fruit."

In his personal letter to the Pope, Bernard adroit-ly mentioned his battles against *the lion* — an al-lusion to Pierleone, the antipope — and complained that he had to fight *the dragon* — that is to say, Abelard, whom he compared to Goliath, preceded by his squire Arnold of Brescia. And he added this eloquent plea:

"It is now up to you, Peter's successor, to judge if the man who attacks the faith should find refuge close to the chair of Peter!"

But Bernard did not stop there. He had under-stood the weight that might be attached to the words of young Hyacinth Orsini, and feared the Pope might be listening to unwise counselors. It has been esti-mated that Bernard wrote not less than ten letters, each more pressing than the last, to warn the cardinals against Abelard's doctrines. He denounced Abelard as a most dangerous man who prided himself in having supporters at the Roman Court. He did not hesitate to accuse him not only of being a heretic, but even of being "a precursor of Anti-Christ" because of his obstinate defense of his errors and his efforts to propagate them. Bernard asked: *"Who will rise to silence this deceiver?... Is there no one who suffers personally from insults made to Christ?"*

It is obvious that Bernard saw Abelard's teachings as an extreme danger to the Church. Abelard, for his part, assured by his young friend Hyacinth, believed and claimed that the cardinals were for him. Later on, we shall show that the abbot of Clairvaux did not have great confidence in some of the cardinals. This was the reason for his apprehension and for his use of language deemed by some to be intemperate. However, no one can doubt his complete sincerity and deep awareness of the danger facing the Church in this circumstance.

Rome's Verdict

Meanwhile, Abelard had been busy for his cause. He had prepared a confession of faith for the Pope's use. And in this profession that he considered beyond attack, he accused the abbot of Clairvaux of "ignorance, falsification, and hysteria."

While Bernard had denounced him as "the precursor of Anti-Christ," he in turn denounced Bernard as a devil masquerading as an angel of light. It has been said that the quarrels among theologians are the more virulent of all. That is perhaps an exaggeration when they are compared to political and financial quarrels. But no one can deny it is easy to exceed the limits of reason in the name of zeal for the faith. In the present instance, we shall see that everything worked out better than could have been hoped.

Abelard was the first to acknowledge he had gone too far. He had a profound change of heart. He learned that Héloïse, his one-time friend who had become a nun, was greatly disturbed by all the talk about him. He then sent her a letter whose tone was very different from his former arrogance. It is in this letter that we find the sentence cited earlier: "I don't want to be a philosopher who contradicts St. Paul; nor an Aristotle, separated from Christ. For there is no other name under heaven in which I can find my salvation."

Now that Abelard's resolve to remain faithful always to his faith in Jesus Christ had brought him peace of soul, he set out for Rome. But he did not have to go all the way. As he was passing through Cluny, he decided to seek the counsel of Peter the Venerable, who was highly regarded by everyone. While he was there, the news suddenly broke that the Pope had spoken.

The Pope had pronounced his verdict, and it was favorable to Bernard's view, to the judgment of the Council of Sens, and against Abelard. Bernard's many letters had borne fruit. Innocent II did indeed consult the Sacred College, as was customary in such cases. We do not know whether he found a single defender of Abelard's writings among the cardinals. Contrary to custom, Rome passed judgment very quickly. The answer to the archbishops of Sens and Rheims, as well as to Bernard was dated July 16, 1140, not more than six weeks after the Council of Sens had issued its decision.

The Pope said in part: "Therefore, having sought the counsel of our brothers the bishops and cardinals, we, by virtue of the authority of the sacred canons, condemn the articles gathered by your efforts and all the perverse dogmas of Peter, as well as the author himself, and we impose perpetual silence upon him, as being a heretic."

In a second pontifical letter of the same date, it was ordered that Abelard and his disciple, Arnold of Brescia, be imprisoned separately as "fabricators of perverse dogmas attacking the Catholic faith." Moreover, their books were to be burned, and the Pope personally ordered them to be publicly burned at St. Peter's in Rome.

In actual fact, Abelard managed to escape the rigors of this sentence, and Arnold of Brescia likewise. But they did so by very different methods. Abelard, no doubt mellowed and enlightened by the wisdom of Peter the Venerable, renounced any further efforts to defend himself. Better still, he agreed to talk with Bernard and be reconciled with him. Bernard succeeded in persuading him to condemn all his errors. Instead of being imprisoned in an ecclesiastical prison, he asked to be allowed to spend the rest of his life among the monks of Cluny, whom he edified by his devotion and observance of the rule. Peter the Venerable later compared him to St. Germain for his humility, and to St. Martin for his poverty.

However, Abelard retained his love for study, and the monks of Cluny were happy to learn from him. Unfortunately, the climate at Cluny was bad for Abelard's health. He had to be sent to the priory of St.-Marcel near Châlon-sur-Saône. There, again, he engaged in his passionate love of reading. He prayed, dictated, wrote. But his illness worsened. On April 21, 1142, less than two years after his condemnation, Abelard died peacefully in the Lord. He was sixty-three years old, the same age Bernard was to die eleven years later.

Although Abelard left no school, no system of thought to posterity, he was nevertheless a precursor of the great scholastics. His method of *Sic et Non* was adopted by St. Thomas Aquinas, who consistently presented pros and cons in his *Summa Theolo-*

gica, possible objections and answers to them. These words *Sic et Non* mean *Yes and No.* Under this title, Abelard had gathered a large number of apparently contradictory texts, to prove that the truth lies in the "golden mean."

Bernard's Treatises

This formidable quarrel stirred up the entire Church. It alone would have sufficed to win for Bernard consideration as an eminent "doctor," since he finally triumphed over the most brilliant philosopher of his century. But he has other claims to our admiration in the realm of theology. Two of his treatises in particular deserve our attention. The first concerns love of God and is entitled *De diligendo Deo—On the Duty of Loving God.* The second is devoted to the study of the delicate problem of grace and free will: *De Gratia et libero Arbitrio.*

Without analyzing these two works in detail, we shall speak of them briefly here.

In the matter of love of God, Bernard teaches, following all the Church Fathers and the Gospel, that it was God who first loved us. He has expressed his view in this overall concept:

"God offers us His merits; He reserves Himself as our reward; He gives Himself as food to holy souls; He surrenders Himself for the redemption of captive souls."

And also:

"What shall I render to the Lord for all that He has given me? In His first work—creation—He gave me to myself;—in the second—sanctification—He gives Himself to me; and in giving Himself He has given me back to myself. Given and returned to myself, I owe myself totally to Him and I owe myself to Him twice! But what shall I return to God for giving Himself to me?—For, even if it were possible to give myself a thousand times, what am I, in comparison with God?"

It is in this work and in the context we have briefly outlined that Bernard's famous words are to be found:

"The reason for loving God is God Himself; and the measure of our love for Him is to love Him without measure."

We can see how deeply he was immersed in such thoughts when we read the following commentary:

"Is it possible? Immensity loves us! Eternity loves us! Incomprehensible Love loves us!—God loves us! He whose greatness has no limits, whose wisdom is unbounded, whose peace exceeds all sentiment. And we in return, would measure out our love to Him! Oh Lord! My strength and my support, my liberator, my all that is most adorable, most loving, I shall love You, my God, according to Your gift and to my measure, most certainly less than You deserve, but as much as I can; for even though I cannot love You as much as I ought, I still do not owe greater love than I am capable of giving!" (*De diligendo Deo*, I, I and VI, 16)

Bernard's second treatise mentioned above on *Grace and Free Will* reminds us of St. Augustine who had already written magnificently on the same subject. One day, when Bernard was explaining St. Augustine's statement that "man's merits are simply God's gifts," someone asked him: "But if God is the author of every good thing we do, what hope have we of obtaining a reward?"

It was in answer to this question that Bernard wrote his treatise. He started right out with the question: "What is it that saves?" And he answered:

"It is grace. What then of free will? I answer briefly: it is saved! In fact, take away free will, and there is nothing to save; take away grace, and there is nothing that saves. Both are necessary to salvation. One receives, the other produces the effect."

Bernard then went on to define free will as *"a power of the reason and of the will."* And he added:

"It is called 'free' in relation to the volition which can turn in one direction or another; and it is named 'will' in relation to reason which has the power to discern."

Thus, Bernard was refuting the error of Luther and Calvin four hundred years before the fact. For he taught that man's will remains free *"even after the fall,"* but is powerless in the order of supernatural good. To quote him again:

"Volition is in us by virtue of free will: I say volition and not willing good or willing evil. It is free will that makes us will, but it is grace that makes us will the good: *liberum arbitrium nos facit volentes, gratia benevolos....* In this matter, what is the merit of the will? It lies in consent."

This consent comes from God also, but "it cannot occur without our cooperation." And that is why God attributes it to us as a merit.

As we can readily see, Bernard's doctrine of grace reproduces St. Augustine's with perfect accuracy. Long before the errors of Protestantism, Baianism and Jansenism, Bernard had refuted them. It is therefore with good reason that he is included among the Doctors of the Church.

Bernard and the Immaculate Conception

On one point, however, Bernard was mistaken. True, he erred in very good company, for his error on the doctrine of the Immaculate Conception of Mary was shared by Thomas Aquinas and Bonaventure.

How is it these great intellects did not see that the Immaculate Conception, that is, the privilege of being preserved from original sin, could not be separated from the title of Mother of God? It seems they reasoned along these lines:

Mary, inasmuch as she is the Mother of God, must be granted all that it is possible to attribute to her, but she cannot be separated from her Divine Son, the universal Redeemer. To claim Mary is exempt from original sin is to deprive her of the honor of having been purified, as we have, in the blood of Jesus. It is to see her as further removed from Jesus the Savior than we are.

But the answer to this objection is this: not only does the Immaculate Conception not separate Mary from the Redeemer, but it places her in a state of friendship with her Jesus far more perfect than ours. For there are two ways of being redeemed: the ordinary way, which is to be redeemed after having been subjected to the fall; and then there is the perfect way, which is to have been *preserved* from the fall. In other words, Mary was redeemed more completely and perfectly than all other human beings, for she was conceived without sin through the anticipated merits of her Divine Son.

But let us come back to Bernard. As we have said, he was the bard, the lute-player, the knight of our Blessed Lady. So true is this, that many of our most beautiful prayers to Mary have been attributed to him, although his authorship has not been proven. Among these great hymns of praise to the Mother of God are the *Alma Redemptoris Mater,* the *Ave Regina,* and the *Salve Regina.* Modern scholars have tended to deny his authorship even of the three invocations that close the *Hail Holy Queen:* "O clement, O loving, O sweet Virgin Mary!"

We are closer to the truth when we attribute the *Memorare* to St. Bernard, although perhaps not in its present form. This prayer was composed of invocations taken from his writings, and that is enough to give him the honor of having written it.

The fact remains, however, that Bernard did all in his power to prevent the spread of belief in Mary's Immaculate Conception.

Why? In the first place, he did not think this belief was sufficiently rooted in the essential tenets of the Church and its traditions. Secondly, he thought this teaching had no sound theological basis, as we shall explain.

On the first point, concerning the origin of the honor given to the Immaculate Conception, there was room for doubt. The feast of the Conception of Mary had appeared in the Church in England about a century earlier. It had been temporarily eclipsed at the time of the Norman conquest of England in 1066. But it soon regained popularity under the impetus of the abbot of Canterbury who was one of St. Anselm's nephews, as well as of Osbert of Clare, a monk and prior of Westminster, and of Hugo of Amiens, abbot of Reading, later to become the Archbishop of Rouen.

Apparently, from England the celebration of this feast was brought into Normandy, because it was afterwards called "the feast of the Normans."

It is not clear how this feast, so little known on the continent of Europe, was adopted by the Church of Lyons. This Church wielded so much influence that its acceptance of the feast could not pass unnoticed. When Bernard heard about it, he was greatly disturbed. He knew the feast was not celebrated in Rome, the Mother of all the Churches. As far as he knew, only a few abbeys and unimportant churches observed this feast. He rejected as doubtful certain legends according to which the Blessed Virgin Mary had appeared to a monk who was crossing the English Channel in a dangerous storm. She had rescued him, so it was said, but on condition that he have her Immaculate Conception celebrated on December 8th.

Bernard looked upon these innovations as the actions of "simple" souls who should not be taken too seriously. And he decided to make a careful study of this theological question.

As he saw it, it was argued that the Conception of Mary should be honored because her birth was surely a holy event. He agreed on this point, but rejected the conclusion drawn from this premise. In that case, he said, we should also honor Mary's father and mother. And where would it all end?

Up to this point, Bernard is not very convincing. Nor is he in the further conclusions to which his reasoning led him. Bernard argued that the Blessed Virgin could not have been sanctified at the same moment she was conceived. And why not? Because she could not have been holy before she existed, and no one will argue with that. But Bernard felt her holiness could not be "mixed in" with her conception. And so we come face-to-face with the problem.

Bernard would not admit that reason could accept a simultaneous sanctification and conception. To his mind, every conception is stained with concupiscence, and therefore original sin presides over it. How could the Holy Spirit be present where there is sin? Therefore Mary could have been sanctified *after her conception,* and in her mother's womb, as is generally agreed of John the Baptizer. But she could not have been conceived without sin.

Now, this line of reasoning had already been refuted by Osbert of Clare, one of the original promoters of the feast. For he had distinguished between active and passive conception. He readily admitted that Mary, like all of Adam's children, was necessarily subject to original sin. But by virtue of the future merits of her Divine Son, she had been exempt from original sin. This unique privilege was bound up with her future title of Mother of God. And Osbert of Clare had firmly proclaimed, anticipating his compatriot Duns Scotus, the great Franciscan theologian, that the feast of the Immaculate Conception celebrates "the firstfruits [we might say, the dawn] of our Redemption."

So, we must not say, as Bernard did, that Mary was *purified* of original sin, but that she was *exempted* or *preserved* from original sin.

Neither Bernard's opposition, nor the opposition of Thomas Aquinas and Bonaventure, stopped the movement of Catholic thinking because it was deep and right. The feast of the Immaculate Conception prevailed. In France, the famous Sorbonne, the University of Paris, placed its doctors under obligation to profess this dogma. The famous Jesuit Father Maldonat was even expelled from Paris and from France for refusing to do so.

For all that, let us not forget that Bernard, no less than Thomas Aquinas and Bonaventure, was a most devoted servant of Mary. He sang the praises of her virginity, he honored her virtues, and above all her humility, and he saw her as the mediatrix of all graces.

In one of his most beautiful sermons, he spoke these decisive words: *"It has been God's will that we should not have anything that had not passed through the hands of Mary"* (In Vig. Nativ. Christi, Sermo III, 10).

Mary is the canal, the aqueduct, by which the waters of heaven come within us. *"Full of grace for herself, she is overflowing and superabundant with grace for us."*

It is certain that Bernard was one of the most powerful propagators of devotion to the Blessed Virgin Mary, and in this respect also he was a Doctor of the Church.

VI

DEFENDER OF CHRISTENDOM

Two Kinds of Enemies

Not only was Bernard the most eminent doctor of the Church in his century. He was also the defender of Christendom against enemies who were threatening its very existence. These enemies were of two kinds: the enemies within, and the enemies on the outside. The latter, of course, were the unbelievers, the Moslems. We shall talk about them later.

The enemies within the Christian world were of a totally different sort. They worked in the shadows, they deceived the faithful by their malicious sermons. They spread the most extravagant notions. We know little about them except from the authors of chronicles who have recorded the battles fought against them.

First there had been a certain Tanchelin, whose disastrous propaganda first spread in the diocese of Utrecht, and thence to the dioceses of Antwerp, Cambrai, and Liège. His heresy attacked the Christian hierarchy, denying all authority to the Pope and the bishops, and leading to the most cynical depravity. Tanchelin had gone so far as to publicly proclaim his betrothal to the Blessed Virgin Mary, as though with the intention of sullying her virginity. Tanchelin had some measure of success, but St. Norbert fought him with great energy. In the end, Tanchelin was killed in 1115 by an exasperated priest.

Ideas similar to those of Tanchelin were being spread among the weavers of the province of Champagne and as far as the Rhine. These notions seemed akin to the ancient Manichaeism, as St. Augustine has described it. Some monks and clerics had joined this secret sect. In 1143, the archbishop of Cologne had brought a few of these heretics before a tribunal. The president of the court, who was the provost of Steinfeld, suggested that Bernard of Clairvaux be called in to help fight this peril to the Christian world.

Bernard's Influence

We know that whenever Bernard was not obliged to leave his cloister in obedience, he devoted himself diligently to the duties of his monastic vocation. We also know that sometime around the year 1135, he began the series of sermons on *The Song of Songs*. He had just reached the commentary on the verse: "Catch us the foxes, the little foxes that damage the vineyards" (*The Song of Songs*, 2:15). His discourses were carefully copied and sent to the many monasteries already founded by Clairvaux, where they were eagerly awaited.

Bernard saw in these "little foxes" the image of the wily heretics who were very clever in making incursions into the Lord's vineyard. And he determined to make thorough inquiry into their doctrines and activities. His investigation convinced him of the seriousness of the danger. It is from his own writings that we have the best record of what was involved.

The dissidents were of many nuances and varieties. But they all rejected the authority of the Church.

They claimed it was corrupt and unworthy of its origins. Some of them called themselves the "Apostolics," as though to set themselves up as the direct heirs of St. Peter and the apostles. An embryonic hierarchy sometimes existed in these groups, as would later happen among the Albigensians. In fact, they may have been ancestors or in any case precursors of the Albigensians.

Thus, some were the "elect," the leaders, and the rest were "hearers," or disciples. They admitted the Bible as the source of their faith, but a Bible they had mutilated. Actually, they rejected the entire Old Testament, and some of them also rejected a few of St. Paul's Epistles. But they tended most often to ridicule the baptism of infants, purgatory, prayers for the dead, the communion of saints, and most of the sacraments. They would indeed receive the sacraments like everyone else, in order to conceal their identity from true Catholics, but they denied the sacraments had any value or efficacy.

In the domain of morals, the "elect" affected an almost superhuman strictness, which many thought to be just a mask. For one of their axioms was said to be: "Swear, perjure yourself, but never reveal the secret!" Bernard never believed they were virtuous, in spite of appearances to the contrary.

Bernard's suspicions seemed to have been justified by the fact that although they held marriage in contempt, there was not one of these men who didn't have a woman in his home, using the excuse that the apostles had done the same.

Once Bernard had all the facts, he joined battle. He began by fighting from his cloister, through his Sermons on *The Song of Songs* (especially his Sermons 64 to 66). As these sermons were widely read, their effect was to put Christians on their guard.

Bernard's initial attack was against the heretics' scorn for the sacrament of matrimony:

"One must be brutish not to see that to condemn valid marriage is to open the way to every sort of lewdness. Snatch from the Church honorable marriage and the sinless marriage bed and you will fill the Church with concubinage, incest, and unclean beings. Make your choice: either people heaven with these monsters or reduce the number of the elect to those alone who are continent. But continence is rare on this earth. How can anyone believe that the Savior humbled and abased Himself for them alone? How could all of us have received the plenitude of His grace, if only the continent share in it? By what right can anyone thus shorten the arm of God?"

And as the heretics claimed to be practicing absolute continence while living in the company of women, Bernard asked them this question:

"Tell me, my friend, who is this woman I see by your side? Is it your wife? No, you say, I have made a vow not to have one! Is it your daughter? Again, no! Well then, who is it? A sister, a niece, or indeed a relative more or less removed? Not at all.

"But then, how can your virtue be secure in such company?... This young girl is in close contact with you every day, and you want me to believe in your virtue! Let us admit that you are chaste. But this intimacy is still not permissible to you. If you don't know it, learn that the Church forbids cohabitation of men and women who have made a vow of continence. If you do not want to scandalize the Church, then send this woman away!"

To understand the full force of these arguments, we must remember that this was written at the height of what has been called "the Gregorian Reform." The Church had been obliged to fight for the dignity of its members, and especially of its clergy. Bernard was in complete accord with this powerful reform, which the ecumenical councils of 1123 and 1139 confirmed and made obligatory.

Bernard could not help wondering in what measure his castigations would be heeded. He knew that most of the heretics he was addressing were ignorant, spread out over the countryside — *rusticani et idiotae* — as he used to say.

He also knew that *"faith can be given, but it cannot be forced on anyone."* In his Sermon 64, he criticized those who put heretics to death, thus making them *"martyrs of perfidy."*

And yet, in his Sermon 66, he came to a terrifying conclusion:

"They cannot be convinced by reasons, for they do not understand them. They cannot be reprimanded by persons in authority, for they acknowledge no authority. They cannot be moved by persuasion, because they are obdurate. The proof is clear: they prefer to die than to be converted. Nothing is left for them but the stake!"

But these words should not make us suppose Bernard approved the burning of impenitent heretics, which was to be a common, and even more lamentably, a legal occurrence toward the end of the twelfth century. But there had already been executions by popular demand, so to speak. These had taken place in Orleans, Arras, and Soissons. More recently, the people of Cologne, Germany, had attacked heretics as they stood before the tribunal. Infuriated by the heretics' stubbornness, and despite the judges' opposition, they had seized the defendants and cast them upon a pyre where they were burned to death.

Bernard called this incident to mind in his Sermon 65. But he pointed out that the people's fury had only succeeded in creating false martyrs. They had gone to excesses. *"While we approve their zeal, we in no sense approve what they have done."*

Bernard unreservedly condemned the bishops who, through negligence or indifference, allowed the "foxes" to ravage the Lord's vineyard. He wanted them to search them out, stop them, and try to educate them in the truth. Only those heretics who stubbornly persisted in their views would be excommunicated and turned over to the secular authorities. As Bernard saw it, the Church's task was to convince. The state's task was to repress abuses.

Bernard in Languedoc

The time came when Bernard had to leave the peace of his monastery once more and preach against new heretics of a more dangerous sort.

Heresy was spreading rapidly in southern France. Its propagators were Peter of Bruys and his disciple Henry of Lausanne. The former is known to us only through Peter the Venerable and Bernard. It is thought he was burned at the stake sometime between 1139 and 1143. More is known about Henry of Lausanne, although we do not know much about his early years. One chronicle claims he was a hermit. Bernard thought he had been a monk who later became an apostate. Another author referred to him as a former "black monk" or member of the Cluniac Order.

According to Bernard, Henry was a "scholarly" man—*litteratus.* He had even received permission to preach from the bishop of Le Mans. But he had immediately abused it. Under an austere exterior, he was a man of coarse and perverted appetites. He impressed the common people by his tall stature, his melodious voice, his quick glance, his long beard and bare feet. It was known he depended entirely on alms for his livelihood and slept on the hard ground. Young men and women were especially drawn to him. However, he soon caused a scandal, and it was clear that there was in him a dangerous, impure mixture of mysticism and debauchery.

Henry of Lausanne seems to have been a precursor of the Quietists, in the sense that he imagined that just because he claimed to be God's friend he had the right to all sorts of moral liberties. When the bishop of Le Mans was told about it upon his return from a trip to Rome, he discreetly sent him away from his diocese. It is thought Henry then went toward Poitou and Aquitaine.

In 1135 Henry was arrested upon the order of the Archbishop of Arles, and was summoned before the Council of Pisa, where he abjured his errors. Everyone thought he was converted. Bernard even invited him to Clairvaux. But Henry did not keep his promises. He was then about sixty-five years old, and the thought of living a monastic life frightened him. In any event, he resumed his peregrinations, and adopted the ideas of Peter of Bruys, becoming his disciple in 1139.

What is known of Henry's doctrine as of this date? In the first place, he appealed to the Gospel and rejected the authority of the Church. Secondly, he rejected the practice of baptizing infants, and was hostile to the Mass, the Eucharist, the communion of saints, and prayers for the deceased. By this very fact, he abolished the ecclesiastical hierarchy, and together with it, divine worship, the liturgy, religious hymns, and churches. Going still further, he invited the people to despoil the clergy, by seizing their property, and to pillage and even demolish churches.

It is generally believed that Peter of Bruys was burned by an angry mob because he had built a pyre with crosses from churches. Perhaps Henry spared the crosses, out of fear of the people's ire, but he remained deeply hostile to the clergy and to the Christian tradition. He preached an easy religion, and found ready listeners not only among the common people but also among some of the nobility. His coarse jokes were often greeted with guffaws. The extent of his influence can be measured by Bernard's complaints:

"What have we learned and what are we learning each day? The heretic Henry has done and continues to do great wrong to the Church of God! The basilicas are without faithful, the faithful are without priests, and priests are without honor! In a word, now there are only Christians without Christ!" (Letter 241)

In fact, in a large area of Languedoc in southwestern France, the churches were empty. No one received the sacraments. Children were no longer baptized. "O sorrow! Is such a man to be listened to and will a whole people believe in him?"

This was surely reason enough for Bernard to come out of his beloved monastery once more. He was to a certain extent obliged to do so by the insistence of the Pope's legate, Alberic, Cardinal-Bishop of Ostia.

The Campaign of 1145

Bernard was then fifty-five years old. His health, which had never been very robust, was now shattered. However, he set out in the month of May, 1145. When he reached Poitiers he was so exhausted that he was almost ready to give up his journey. But as an early biographer of Bernard recounts, he was encouraged from within, by heavenly consolations that gave him wings. And soon he was on his way to Bordeaux, by way of Angoulême and Limoges. He arrived at his destination on June 1st, and had the joy of reconciling the bishop of Bordeaux with his canons. With the bishops of the area, he organized missions into Languedoc. Bernard wrote to the Count of Toulouse, saying:

"Although I am completely infirm in body, I come into this land where the savage Henry is wreaking his ravages. After being driven out of all of France, he found asylum in your domains and is unleashing his fury against the flock of Christ. It is for you to decide, illustrious prince, whether this befits your honor or not. Besides, I am not surprised that this wily serpent has been able to deceive you, for, while he does not possess the virtue of piety, he gives all the appearances of having it."

Bernard did not want to accuse lightly the man he had come to fight. He advised the count to make inquiries in the places where the heretic was known —Lausanne, Le Mans, and Poitiers. All serious witnesses affirmed that this apostate was nothing but a hypocrite, whose private life was most scandalous.

After sending his letter off to the Count of Toulouse, Bernard set out in the direction of Bergerac, Perigueux, and Cahors. His reputation was such that everywhere he went crowds came to hear him. The fickle populations of these regions soon were turned around and reconquered. At Sarlat, he worked a miracle that made a great impression on everyone. And finally he reached Toulouse, where he was received with so much enthusiasm that Henry the heretic thought it best to slip away.

Henry's departure caused some dismay among his partisans, who were mostly weavers, merchants, and dissipated young nobles. The easy religion Henry was preaching suited them so well that they were reluctant to renounce it. But, they still had a little faith left deep in their souls, and Bernard appealed to it in his sermons. He held up the Christian faith of the entire Catholic Church against the distorted and truncated belief the fugitive had been preaching.

Bernard asked: Why was Henry not there to defend his ideas? Was not his flight an admission of guilt? And wasn't what was known about this vagabond monk proof enough of his unworthiness? Bernard's public revelations on this matter were so convincing that many of his hearers were ashamed of their master, abandoned his cause, and were converted.

However, Bernard's success was only partial. There was still some obstinate resistance. Bernard turned to God and asked Him to make His light shine on this people by giving some sign. His prayer was answered, for he worked the miraculous cure of a canon in Toulouse under circumstances that filled the whole city with admiration.

The dying canon had stood up at Bernard's words. Everyone rushed up to acclaim the man who had cured him. Bernard, who hated noisy demonstrations, refused to appear before the enthusiastic crowd. But everyone knew he would continue his preaching. So the next time he stood in the pulpit he found an eager audience, whom he easily won over. The people of Toulouse were converted in droves, and pledged themselves under oath to break off all contact with Henry of Lausanne and his partisans.

This was not the last of Bernard's victories in southern France. He decided to go to Albi. On the way, he passed through Verfeil, a village completely lost to heresy. The inhabitants refused to listen to him. The holy abbot was obliged to pronounce an anathema against the entire village. According to the chronicler William of Puylaurens, Bernard spoke with such force that when Dominic Guzman came to this area a century later, he discovered the richest families of Verfeil had been ruined as a consequence of their rebellion against Bernard.

Finally, on June 28, 1145, Bernard arrived in Albi. His mission did not begin well. His first companions had been received very coldly. Nonetheless, when Bernard appeared in person and especially when he began to speak, refuting the heresy and calling upon the people to make a choice between truth and error, there was a great wave of enthusiasm in the audience. Many returned to the fold.

About this time Bernard received several letters urgently recalling him to Clairvaux, and was obliged to shorten his stay in Languedoc. As one early biographer has said, it would have been far better for him to continue the campaign in southern France. But Bernard's first obligation was to his beloved monastery, where his presence was really needed. He therefore gave up this campaign after a few months. Soon after his return to Clairvaux, he was delighted to hear that Henry the heretic had been arrested. Nothing more was heard of him. It is assumed he was kept in prison until he died, and his partisans showed little concern over his fate. Several centuries later, certain Protestants came to look upon Henry of Lausanne as a precursor of the Protestant Reformation.

It does not seem likely that any serious modern historian, whether Protestant or Catholic, would think of rehabilitating a man as suspect as Henry of Lausanne and hold him up against a man like Bernard. No one can deny the Church counted among its members, and even among its clergy, men who did not do honor to their faith. Bernard was to see this very clearly and to be a great reformer in this regard. In any event, the cause Bernard defended against Henry of Lausanne was truly God's cause.

When Bernard received the news from Languedoc about Henry's arrest, he thought the heresy had been quashed. He wrote to the people of Toulouse, giving them extensive advice. Lausanne's heresy did in fact die out, but only to give way in later years to the Albigensian heresy. But by that time there would be another saint to follow Bernard's zealous example: Dominic Guzman. Now we must turn our attention to our hero's warfare against the infidels in the Holy Land.

Jerusalem

While Bernard kept his eyes focused on Rome, as the capital of the Christian world, he was too much aware of the Church's needs not to turn his attention toward Jerusalem and the Holy Land. He was still very young when the brave knights of the First Crusade captured the city that had been the birthplace of Christianity. As a boy of nine, he had rejoiced with all of Christ's disciples over the deliverance of Jerusalem.

During the first years of his abbacy, in 1128, he had been asked to help write the Rule for the Order of the Knights Templars. He had made a point of recommending to these knights of God who "placed their lives at the service of their brothers" either the patriarchs of Jerusalem and Antioch, or Queen Melisande. His zeal had been rewarded by the gift of a fragment of the true Cross sent to him by the patriarch of Jerusalem.

For a long time Bernard seemed to have no anxiety about the Christian Kingdom of Jerusalem. And yet the Moslem peril continued, not only in Syria and Palestine, but also in Spain. The Moslem, that is to say, the Turkish threat had become increasingly serious since the year 1111. But suddenly, in 1144, it assumed terrifying proportions.

On November 28, 1144, the Atabek of Mosul, Imad-ed-Din-Zenki, appeared before the city of Edessa. Before the Christians of Antioch and Jerusalem had time to come to the rescue, he captured the city, delivered it to pillage, and completely destroyed it. This occurred on Christmas day, 1144. The blow was felt by all the Latin lords in Palestine. There was a sort of panic, as if the death-knell had rung for all Christian holdings in that part of the world. Bishop Hugo of Gabala was hastily sent to Rome to ask the Pope for help, and through him, to ask help of the whole Western world.

As it happened, since February 15, 1145, the Pope was a disciple of St. Bernard and a former Cistercian monk. He had taken the name of Eugene III.

It has sometimes been said that the Pope, who had been driven out of Rome by the disorders provoked by the agitator Arnold of Brescia, had done very little when first told of the perils threatening Christian Palestine. That is certainly not true. On the contrary, he was deeply disturbed and set to work at once to meet the situation. A proof of it is that he addressed a bull to Louis VII, King of France, inviting him to take up the cross and set out in person for the Middle East. Although this bull was dated December 1, 1146, recent historical research has proven it was sent a year earlier, on December 1, 1145, and must have reached the French king by December 15, 1145.

The bull arrived at an opportune moment. For the king was a man of deep and sincere faith. Besides, he had bitter remorse over the disaster at Vitry, which had been burned at his command and where 1,300 persons had been killed. He also appears to have received appeals directly from the Middle East.

In any event, King Louis VII chose the occasion of a large gathering of his lords at Bourges on December 25, 1145, to announce his intention of going on a crusade and to invite them to follow his example. Everyone was taken by surprise. But in spite of the exhortations of the bishop of Langres, who was present, the lords showed little enthusiasm to accede to the king's wishes. It even seems that certain important figures such as Suger, the famous abbot of

St.-Denis and the king's closest counselor, raised objections against such a project.

Finally, it was decided at Bourges to hold a second assembly around Easter of the following year, at the abbey of Vézelay, which is about eight miles from Avallon, in the Yonne region of France.

Bernard Preaches the Crusade

The question immediately arose as to who would be chosen to preach this Second Crusade. The choice of the man who was to electrify the crowds and stir their enthusiasm was delicate and important. Neither the king nor the Pope seem to have had the slightest doubt as to who this man should be.

Bernard's name was the first that came to their minds. The king immediately approached him on the matter. This was a great surprise for Bernard, too. While he was deeply interested in Palestine, he had not been told about events in Syria or about Eugene III's bull calling for a crusade. For Bernard did not attend the assembly at Bourges, although some misinformed chroniclers have claimed he did.

First of all, he wanted to be under the orders of the Holy See in this matter. He felt an undertaking as vast as a crusade, to judge by the precedent of Urban II who preached the crusade personally at Clermont-Ferrand in 1095, should be under papal jurisdiction.

In a new bull, dated March 1, 1146, Pope Eugene III renewed his call for a crusade more forcefully and clearly than on the previous December 1st. He also expressed his regret that troubled conditions in Rome prevented him from following the example of his predecessor Urban II. Since he could not "blow the evangelical trumpet" in France, he urged all the faithful of France to take up the cross and invited Bernard to preach in his place.

This time, Bernard could hesitate no longer. The assembly of Vézelay had been convoked for March 31, 1146. He had no time to lose. A vast crowd had gathered. Although the abbey church was very large, it was too small for the occasion. An improvised rostrum was built out in the open, from which Bernard was to preach.

A Memorable Discourse

This was probably one of the greatest sermons Bernard ever preached. Like all great orators, when he began to speak he would forget all his chronic ailments. He was literally transformed. We have no record of the sermon he gave on that occasion. Odo of Deuil, the historian of the crusade, has related that the audience listened with rapture to Bernard's voice which seemed to be coming from heaven, like an angel's. In this chronicler's words, everyone gathered the saint's words "the way the calyx of a flower drinks in the dew."

Bernard began by reading the Pope's bull. He commented on it by giving a report on what was happening in the Holy Land. He stirred his audience by appealing to their faith and their love for Christ. He called to mind the privileges attached to the taking up of the crusader's cross. To all who did so, the Pope granted "absolution and remission of their sins," in other words, a plenary indulgence. In a group of people so full of faith and zeal, such a promise aroused great emotion. Soon the orator was interrupted by shouts from every side:

"*Crosses! Crosses! Give us some crosses!*"

Bernard had to accede to his audience's desires. He stopped his sermon and began to distribute crosses.

To quote Odo of Deuil, "He sowed crosses rather than distributed them. And when the crosses prepared beforehand were all given out, he had to tear his clothes in order to make new ones, which he continued to distribute throughout the day."

Among the crusaders of Vézelay were some very important personages: the Queen of France, Aliénor of Aquitaine; the Count of Dreux, who was the King's brother; Count Alphonsus of Toulouse in whose lands Bernard had preached against the heretics the year before; the sons of the Count of Champagne; the Count of Nevers; and the Count of Flanders.

It goes without saying that the support of each of these powerful noblemen brought with it the support of their vassals. So the newly formed army was to have leaders, and first among them, the King.

Bernard's Labors for the Crusade

But Bernard did not consider his mission finished when he had preached at Vézelay. We have already seen his perseverance in any task he undertook, such as his efforts against the schism of Anacletus. So now he set out to preach the crusade in the various provinces. While we are not able to reconstruct all the details of his itinerary, it is certain that he travelled through Burgundy, Lorraine, and Flanders. And he did not confine himself to preaching, for he wrote many letters to the lords he had not been able to reach in person.

So fiery was his zeal, that in the end he transcended the original intentions of the Holy See.

Now, Pope Eugene III had not intended to extend the preaching of the crusade into Germany. He was counting on the intervention of Conrad III to restore order in Italy and at Rome. But the force of circumstances led Bernard to include Germany in his appeals to join the crusade.

The unexpected events that brought this about were as follows. A Cistercian monk named Rudolph had begun preaching the crusade in the region of Mainz, Cologne, Worms, Speyer, and even Strasbourg. His words were so inflamatory that riots had broken out against the Jews in these areas. The bishops disapproved of such violence, but they didn't know how to stop it. Then the archbishop of Cologne had the good idea of appealing to the prestige of Bernard, who was then preaching in Flanders. Bernard immediately answered the archbishop's call, and we shall now follow him into Germany.

Bernard in Germany

In responding to the invitation to come to Germany, Bernard's first task was to stop the *pogroms,* as these organized massacres against the Jews were to be called in later times. He made the monk Rudolph stop preaching and return to his monastery. Calm was at once restored.

In the meantime, the question of the crusade inevitably came up. Many objections were raised against extending the movement to Germany. Chief of these, as we have just said, was the urgent need of restoring order in Italy. But there was another reason as well. Conrad's right to the German crown was being challenged by certain feudal lords. Besides, he was anxious to be crowned emperor by the Pope, in order to put an end to these oppositions. Instead of turning to Conrad, Bernard first addressed himself to the Rhenish bishops who had sent for him. In one of his letters to these bishops he said:

"Your land is fertile in courageous men and rich in strong young men. The renown of your bravery has spread over the whole world. Gird your loins, take up your glorious arms, for the love and defense of the Christian name.... Warlike spirits, here is an opportunity to conquer without peril. Here, to conquer is glory and to die is gain.... I propose a profitable bargain to you. Take up the cross. Its materials cost very little, but it is of great value. Its price is the Kingdom of God!"

But Bernard soon understood that nothing could be achieved without the German king's support. So he boldly went to see him at Frankfurt on the Main. His first entreaties had no effect. He was on the point of returning to Clairvaux and abandoning his plans to preach a crusade in Germany. But the bishops urged him to stay. He agreed to preach the crusade on the Rhine, at Fribourg, Basle, Schaffhausen, and Constance. Obviously, in these areas, he had to speak through an interpreter. Even then, he had great success, and felt confident his preaching would finally win the king over too.

Conrad had convoked a diet at Speyer at Christmas, 1146, when he was solemnly crowned. Bernard attended. After the coronation, he took advantage of the general excitement to renew his request for a crusade. Conrad still hesitated. Bernard was not discouraged. During a Mass on December 27th, he addressed the following words to the prince: *"O man, what should I have done for you that I have not done?"* He spoke these words as coming from Christ's own lips. This time Conrad could resist no longer, and promised to take up the crusader's cross.

Bernard could now return to his beloved monk's cell, but he did not put the Second Crusade out of his mind. He began to send letters in all directions from Clairvaux. He urged the entire Christian world to take part in the effort against the infidels. He addressed himself to England, Bohemia, Bavaria, Poland, Denmark, Sweden, and Norway.

In his zeal, the abbot of Clairvaux had not considered or even guessed the Pope's intentions. He saw everything in terms of the crusade, whereas the Pope was keeping his eyes on Rome and Italy.

Soon Eugene III came to France and stopped at Clairvaux, on his way to Germany to invite Conrad III to lead an expedition into Italy. When he learned all that Bernard had been doing on his own initiative, he was not pleased. He sent a messenger to Germany to find out what the German king's plans were. But the king had already made his decision. In May, 1147, Conrad left Bamberg for Ratisbonne, and went down the Danube on his way to the Middle East. The Second Crusade had begun.

Meanwhile, the Pope went to Paris, where King Louis VII was also preparing for his departure and had placed the administration of his realm in the hands of Suger. After a final interview with the French king, Eugene III returned to Italy in June, 1147, making stops all along the way.

The Crusade Fails

We cannot follow the course of this crusade in detail. Bernard had played a preponderant role in promoting it, as we have seen. But once the expedition was under way, it no longer depended on him. Now, all he could do was pray, and this he certainly did.

Unfortunately, the leaders of this gigantic undertaking made some very serious mistakes. As had happened at the time of the First Crusade, there were too many pilgrims, both men and women, who mingled with the soldiers and hampered their movements. Besides, adequate preparations had not been made in the diplomatic area. Emperor Manuel I Comnenus in Constantinople thought of the crusade only as a restoration of the Byzantine Empire. So he claimed the right to demand from Conrad and Louis the feudal homage of the reconquered territories. The two kings rejected these childish dreams with indignation.

Relations between the West and Byzantium grew bitter. To make things worse, the crusaders pillaged as they passed through Manuel's lands. Conrad III had been badly received in Constantinople. While Louis VII was given a slightly more cordial reception, his soldiers were so annoyed with the Greeks that the bishop of Langres urged them to capture Constantinople. This is what finally did happen in 1204, during the Fourth Crusade.

Finally, there was no coordination between the French and the Germans. They arrived in successive waves. Exhausted by their long marches, they were overcome by a climate so different from their own and were unprepared to fight the Turks. They realized they could not recapture Edessa, or even reach the city. Conrad in his discouragement returned to his own country. Louis VII, who had brought his Queen, Aliénor, with him, was grieved by her worldly and frivolous behavior. He led his contingents to Jerusalem where he remained until Easter, 1149. Then he, too, returned to the West without having accomplished anything of importance.

Renewed Efforts

Bernard had felt the disappointment of this bitter defeat more than anyone. But could things be allowed to remain as they were? Was not the honor of the Christian name at stake? Suger, who was a very wise man, thought it was. Bernard agreed with him. They decided nothing was irremediably lost, and that everything could be rectified if everyone would only learn from the painful experience. Bernard wrote an urgent letter to Pope Eugene III, to get him to share his view. He said in part:

"Timidity and lukewarmness are not appropriate in such a serious and important matter. I read somewhere that the brave man feels his courage grow with difficulties. Jesus Christ has been wounded in the apple of His eye. He is suffering once more in those places where He suffered long ago. The moment has come to unsheathe the two swords."

Bernard was using the language of his time to designate the Pope's two powers, one in the spiritual realm and the other in the temporal. For he added:

"Both belong to Peter, who must draw them: one with his own hand, and the other by a sign of his intention.... Imitate the zeal of the man whose place you hold.... I hear a voice crying out: 'I go to Jerusalem, to be crucified again.'"

This same letter (Letter 256 in the Collection) announced to the Pope that a council held at Chartres on May 7, 1150, had appointed Bernard to lead the new crusade, and appealed to the Pope to approve or reject this appointment. Eugene III at first hesitated, but finally yielded. In a bull dated June 19, 1150, he ratified the decision made at Chartres.

But in the end the expedition never materialized, and it was no doubt a good thing. For it would probably have failed. Suger died on January 13, 1151, and Bernard thus lost a friend and first-rate organizer. Besides, Bernard's health was failing, and he was to die on August 20, 1153, taking with him to the grave his regrets over the abortive crusade. In his work *De Consideratione,* he gave voice to this chagrin and blamed the crusade's failure on the sins and wickedness of the crusaders! But he never repudiated the great project he had so tirelessly promoted during the years 1146 to 1150.

VII
BERNARD, THE REFORMER

In the Footsteps of Gregory VII

Bernard of Clairvaux's place in what has been called the "Gregorian Reform" has been well described by the historian Augustine Fliche. This reform began during the eleventh century, under the impetus of the monk Hildebrand. When this monk became Pope under the name of Gregory VII (1070-1085), he continued his zealous efforts. The main concern of the reform was to cleanse the clergy of two evils that were corroding it: simony and Nicholaism.

Gregory VII valiantly fought these evils and succeeded in giving the Church a clergy that was once again worthy of it. He saved the episcopate from the temptations of worldliness that marked the life of the nobles of that era. The Gregorian movement was to be continued by the Roman pontiffs with varying degrees of success until the time of Innocent IV and Boniface VIII. While the Popes continued to be deeply concerned with the reform of the Church, they had many other problems to face as well.

More than once papal activity had to focus exclusively on the struggle between the Church and the state, in other words, on the encroachments of the civil power upon the religious power.

While the morals of the clergy were certainly higher than before, they were still far from perfect. St. Bernard was deeply convinced of this, and became the principal champion of the "Gregorian ideas." He was a great reformer of the Church in every area. He even seems to have been rather severe at times, and lacking in moderation. In particular, he looked upon the secular world with intransigent pessimism. One can find many references in his letters and writings that would seem to indicate he thought the monastic life was the only way to save one's soul.

We have already seen how he treated his sister Humbeline when she came to visit him. In one of his sermons, he exclaimed: "All Christians, or almost all, are seeking only their own interest, O my God, and not Yours!" In another sermon he reprimanded the clergy — no doubt excessively — when he said: "It is no longer enough to say the priests are like the people. For the corruption of the people is far from equalling that of the priests" (from a sermon on the conversion of St. Paul).

In order to understand St. Bernard's work as a reformer, it will be helpful first to see how he influenced individuals, and secondly how he influenced groups.

Bernard, the Recruiter of Monks

One aspect of Bernard's activity as a reformer was his zeal to win as many men as he could to the monastic life. As we have said, it sometimes seems as if he thought the salvation of the individual lay in the religious vocation. But we must not lay undue stress on this point. In any event, it is certain no one ever won as many recruits for the monasteries as he.

We have only to remember how his own vocation started. He had not been content to dedicate himself to the stern Cistercian life. He had taken the offensive against his friends who wanted to retain him in the world. And it was he who triumphed. He converted his assailants. He conquered all his brothers, his uncle, his father, several other relatives, and friends, entering Citeaux with thirty companions. But his efforts to win men's souls did not end with this heroic period of his life. A few statistics will prove it conclusively.

In 1115, we saw Bernard leave Citeaux at the command of Abbot Stephen Harding, and found the monastery of Clairvaux with a dozen other monks. By the time of his death in 1153, Clairvaux numbered 700 religious, and had been rebuilt to provide more spacious quarters. The comparison between these two figures — 12 and 700 — is eloquent. And yet it is insignificant compared to the total reality.

Actually, Clairvaux had not been content to increase its facilities. This monastery had branched out in a most extraordinary way. Here are a few figures. During his lifetime Bernard founded no less than 68 daughter houses directly based on Clairvaux. And these daughter monasteries seem to have had many recruits, for most of them quickly branched out too. So, even during Bernard's own lifetime Clairvaux was the fountainhead, directly or indirectly, of 164 abbeys.

So we see that Bernard won vocations by the thousands, whether for his own abbey or for its daughter monasteries. He rarely gave a sermon outside his monastery without bringing back twenty or thirty young men eager to share his life of total dedication to God. His renown attracted souls. His example spoke to the more generous men. The extreme austerity of the Cistercian Rule, far from being an obstacle to these enthusiastic vocations, seems to have been an added incentive. Whether he appeared in public in Paris, Tournai, Châlons-sur-Marne, the Rhenish lands, or anywhere else, he made conquests by the dozens.

If we study the dates when the 68 daughter abbeys of Clairvaux were founded, we discover that the abbey of Troisfontaines in the diocese of Châlons was founded on October 10, 1118, that is, three years after the arduous foundation of Clairvaux. One year later, on October 29, 1119, the second daughter house was established at Fontenay, in the diocese of Autun. It took two more years before the third monastery was founded at Foigny, in the diocese of Laon (now the diocese of Soissons). After that, the growth seemed to slow down.

However, after 1130, when Bernard's fame had risen because of his role in settling the schism of Anacletus, foundations suddenly increased, and came in rapid succession. In 1131, there were three, and in 1132, there were four. In 1135, there were five new foundations, as compared with two in 1134. One of the most fruitful years was 1140, with seven foundations (Cassamario in Italy, L'Arrivours in the diocese of Troyes, Clairmarais in the diocese of Arras, St. John of Tarouca in Portugal, Whiteland in England, St. Paul – Three Fountains in Rome, and still another in Sicily).

After 1140, foundations were made in other countries: Spain, in 1142, 1147, and 1152; Ireland in 1142; Sweden (two monasteries) in 1143; Belgium in 1146; Sardinia in 1149; and Denmark in 1151.

Bernard thus had "sons" – loving, respectful, enthusiastic sons – in almost all of Christendom, and naturally more in France than elsewhere.

But this "reform of individuals" was not his only work of reform. His popularity, the eminent role he had been called to play in the great affairs of the Church, gave him an opportunity to work through his writings for the reform of the clergy and of the faithful.

The Episcopacy

Bernard has set forth his truly Gregorian ideas on the recruitment of bishops and the indispensable virtues of bishops in a letter which is really a treatise. It was addressed to Henry Le Sanglier, Archbishop of Rheims. As Bernard saw it, a bishop's virtues are chastity, charity, and humility. But whereas Gregory VII had given first place to chastity, Bernard ranked charity far above chastity. For, said he, in this text "Chastity [without charity] is a lamp without oil" (De moribus et officio episcoporum — On the morals and function of bishops, Patrologia Latina, Vol. 182, col. 809-834).

But Bernard also considered humility most necessary to bishops, and bluntly criticized the display of luxury by bishops and abbots of certain wealthy monasteries who lived like great lords. He saw this luxury as a "love of vanity," "effeminateness." Addressing these bishops and abbots, he exclaimed: "Why do you wear women's adornments if you do not want to be criticized the way they are?... If you don't want to be treated like women, stop committing the same sin as they: distinguish yourselves by your works and not by your embroideries and furs...."

Bernard stood out in his century like a prophet of ancient times. He spoke with the power of an Isaiah, a Jeremiah, or a John the Baptizer. He sounded like a social reformer when he spoke of the poor in these terms (in the above-mentioned letter):

"Your superfluity is our very life. Everything that is added to your vanities is a theft from our needs. Your horses prance about weighed down with precious stones, and you pay no heed to our naked limbs."

Such passages were not rare in Bernard's writings. He knew how to be sarcastic and mordant when he wanted to. And he condemned the ambition of the clergy as forcefully as their love of luxury. Still in the same letter, he said:

"Oh! What boundless ambition! There are many among the clergy, of every age and order, learned and ignorant, who rush to obtain ecclesiastical posts, as if, once they obtained such a post they didn't have to worry about anything!...

"For example, as soon as a cleric has become dean, or provost, or archdeacon of a church, he is dissatisfied with having only one dignity and strives to acquire several, both in this church and in others. If the occasion presents itself, he prefers the episcopal dignity to all of these titles. Will he then be satiated? Once he is a bishop, he wants to be an archbishop. If he achieves this, he keeps dreaming of something still higher. He is ready to undertake tiresome journeys and dazzle the familiars of the Roman Court with his lavishness, and thus win costly friendships there!"

A Model Bishop

Let us not imagine that all the bishops of the twelfth century were guilty of such misconduct. Bernard knew some holy prelates, and was their friend and counselor, William of Champeaux among them. But the bishop he esteemed most highly was the Irish bishop St. Malachy, whose biography he wrote.

A life of St. Bernard is incomplete without some mention of the great Irish saint who was his intimate confidant and friend. It was in October, 1148, that Clairvaux welcomed the legate of Ireland, Malachy O'Morgair, a former archbishop of Armagh, who had stepped down to accept the humbler see of Down.

Malachy was born in 1094 or 1095, of devout Christian parents. While still very young he turned for guidance to a famous contemplative hermit named

Imhar, a great admirer of the Gregorian Reform. He saw salvation only through Rome, and Malachy learned great loyalty to the Holy See from him. Malachy then worked with the archbishop of Armagh to reform the Church in Ireland. The religious condition of that land was lamentable. Ancient Irish customs had overshadowed Christianity. The sacraments, and especially marriage, were neglected. The bishoprics had become family estates.

Malachy had worked hard to enforce on his island the laws that had been in force throughout the Church since the Gregorian Reform. When he became archbishop of Armagh, he restored Christian order to some extent. It was then he gave up his high functions to become bishop of a more modest see, Down, thus giving the example of a humility contrary to the ambition Bernard was denouncing.

Malachy first stopped at Clairvaux in 1139 on his way to Rome. Bernard met him and was immediately drawn to him. He would later say of Malachy: "Though he was poor where he himself was concerned, he was rich toward the poor."

And also:

"I have had the privilege of seeing this man: I have benefited from seeing and hearing him. And though I am a sinner, I found favor in his eyes. Our brothers and he edified one another; he gave us a place deep in his heart."

Bernard developed great admiration for Malachy, the man of prayer and penance. For his part, this holy man was so delighted with the spirit of Clairvaux that when he arrived in Rome, the first thing he did was to ask the Pope for the permission to live and die at Clairvaux. But instead, the Pope entrusted him with a new mission of reform in Ireland. Malachy obeyed.

It was only after completing this task that Malachy made his second and last visit to Clairvaux, in 1148.

But on October 18th, the feast of St. Luke, he was felled with a fever that gave him a foreboding of death.

Bernard later wrote: "We all suffered with him in his sickness." As the monks hovered around him attentively, the Irish prelate quietly prophesied: "Nothing will help, but for love of you I'll do whatever you want.... For this very year, Malachy will be stripped of his body." And shortly afterward he said: "The day is near." When he was asked where he would like to die, he answered: "In the very place where our apostle, St. Patrick rests...but if I am going to die in a foreign land, Clairvaux is the place I prefer."

"On what day?" someone insisted.

"The day of the commemoration of all the faithful departed."

All Saints' Day was approaching. Bernard had decided to have the bodies of the deceased monks transferred to a new cemetery adjoining the new church of Clairvaux. Malachy joined in the hymns of the ceremony with great joy, but at the same time, he asked to receive the last sacraments. He even had the strength to go from his cell to the chapel to receive them. Then he returned to his cell with great difficulty and prepared for death. And indeed death came for him on the day he had predicted, as all the monks surrounded him in prayer. While the psalms were being sung, suddenly someone noticed he was no longer moving. His soul had slipped away peacefully. All the monks were convinced they had just witnessed the death of a saint, and felt it was more fitting for them to rejoice than weep.

Bernard gave his friend Malachy the last honors, and kept his tunic as a precious relic. Malachy was buried in the transept of the new convent church.

Bernard decided to write Malachy's biography, pointing to him as a model for bishops to imitate. As a result, his *Life of Saint Malachy* should be considered as a complement to his writings urging the reform of the episcopacy. We should note in passing that Bernard made no mention at all in his biography of Malachy of the list of future Popes included in the famous "Alleged Prophecy of St. Malachy," which later historians were to consider apocryphal. This so-called "prophecy" was actually written by a forger toward the end of the sixteenth century, and is totally fictitious.

Bernard and the Clergy

While Bernard spoke loudly and clearly to the bishops of his time, he was also deeply interested in the lower clergy. He addressed one of his most beautiful sermons to the clergy, which has been published as *"De conversione ad clericos — On conversion for the use of the clergy (Patrologia Latina*, Vol. 182, col. 834-856).

His language in this sermon was in complete accord with the ideals of the Gregorian Reform. He castigated those clerics in particular who were not faithful to the law of ecclesiastical celibacy. He spoke in tones that remind us of St. Peter Damian, who a century earlier had not feared to compare the lives of some clerics to the shame of Sodom and Gomorrah.

Bernard reminded the clergy of something they should never forget: the vanity of the world's pleasures, and especially the pleasures of eating and drinking which slow down the body and too often trouble the mind, leaving only disappointment, remorse, and shame in their wake. The cleric should realize that true joy and consolation are to be found only in God.

So Bernard sought to turn the cleric toward his God, to teach him to see everything in the light of God and do everything for God. The itinerary he offered the members of the clergy of his time was this: break the shackles of the flesh in order to go to God, and then bring God to souls. This is what he meant by the "infusion" and "effusion" of grace, which we mentioned earlier. We can speak convincingly only about the things of which we are full. We must be permeated with God, in order to speak well about God.

Bernard and Lay Society

It is true Bernard's writings often give the impression that he thought salvation was possible only in the cloister. However, his writings addressed to lay persons show that his thought was much more flexible and broader in scope. He spoke to the Christian faithful with zeal. He denounced earthly vanities, the quests of pride and luxury. He gave free play to his pitiless scorn when he described certain coquettish ladies with their rich furs, their earrings studded with precious stones, their gold bracelets that weighed down their arms. He denounced them in their display, showed them up as "adorned and attired like a temple, letting a train of expensive material drag behind them, raising up clouds of dust."

He pointed out how superficial it all was. "Silk, purple, and the false glow of cosmetics probably have a certain beauty, but they do not transmit it. That is beauty applied to one's body and then removed when one undresses!"

But here again what disturbed him most was the contrast between the arrogant wealth of some and the wretched poverty of others. He was convinced

that with all this superfluity it would have been possible to bring effective help to the poor. In his thinking, moral reform led to social reform.

Bernard did not limit himself to condemning
luxury. He was just as stern in his strictures against
idleness, frivolous conversations, and wasted time.
For example, he wrote:

"There is a certain pleasure in conversing just
to pass the time. To pass the time! To while away an
hour! Indeed, this hour that God's mercy grants you
to do penance, to obtain forgiveness, to acquire virtue, to merit the glory promised in the world to come!
This is the time you should spend seeking the favor
of God's power, hastening to join the society of the
angels, sighing for our lost heritage, rousing your lazy
will, weeping over your sins!...

"Would that it pleased the Lord we lost only
the time of earthly life in useless talk! Too often it is
eternal life itself that perishes miserably."

Bernard did not forget that the poor have vices,
too: selfishness, cupidity, jealousy. He could enumer-
ate the duties incumbent upon all men.

Finally, we have proof that Bernard did not want
to oblige everyone to seek salvation in the cloister.
We find it in his sermons on the greatness of Christian
marriage. Of course, he held the view that monks and
nuns ranked above married persons because of "the
holy grandeur of their heroism and purity." But he
certainly did not condemn marriage, as did the
heretics of his day.

In one of his Sermons on *The Song of Songs*, he
said:

"Whoever condemns marriage loosens the reins
on every kind of impurity.... Take this honorable and
uncorrupted sacrament from the Church, and you will
fill it with every sort of debauchery."

He gave useful advice to parents, and spoke with
emotion of paternal and maternal love.

Finally, he described in lyrical terms the benefits of peace in its various aspects:

"Peace of the body is the well-ordered harmony of all its parts. Peace of the irrational soul is the orderly repose of the senses and their appetites. Peace of the rational soul is the harmony between thoughts and actions. Peace of body and soul is the well-ordered life and the salvation of man. Peace of man with God is faith begetting obedience ordered to the divine law. The peace of men is harmony in order. The peace of the home is harmony between the one who commands and those who obey. The peace of the city is similar. The peace of the heavenly city is the most perfectly ordered and the most closely united society possible in the joy of the vision of God. The peace of all things lies in the tranquility of order."

In these last words, we recognize St. Augustine's famous definition.

The "De Consideratione"

It is probable that Bernard, for all his reformer's zeal, would never have dared to become the adviser of Popes, had not one of his sons, a former Italian Cistercian, become Pope Eugene III. This holy monk, whose name was Bernard Paganelli, had been elected to supreme power in the Church on February 15, 1145. From that moment until his death on July 8, 1153, Pope Eugene III and his beloved former teacher were constantly exchanging letters.

Eugene III was to receive the honors of beatification in 1872. It was he who asked Bernard of Clairvaux to prepare for him a book on the duties of the papacy. Bernard finally acceded to his wish, but not without hesitation and apprehension. He seems to have undertaken this task in 1149. It was precisely when the Pontiff, who had been turned into a wanderer by the unrest caused by Arnold of Brescia, had finally returned to Rome. Bernard's book was not completed, however, until 1152 or 1153, when his busy life was almost over. It can be said that in this work Bernard poured all the fruits of his experience and all the treasures stored up in his soul.

What does the title *De consideratione* mean? It is a Pope's examination of conscience. It might be translated: *Matters for a Pope's Consideration,* or perhaps: *A Pope's Major Concerns.*

Bernard saw very clearly that the great danger a Pope faces consists in being submerged by the crush of business. The centralization of the Church resulting from the triumph of the Gregorian ideas had far-reaching effects, but they were not all equally good. The Roman Curia had grown in size and power. The Pope had been obliged to surround himself with many collaborators. Now, some of these men were not always as selfless and holy as they should have been. As we have seen at the time of the schism of Anacletus, certain cardinals nurtured ambitions that were dangerous for the peace of the Church and of the world. Bernard did not mince his words. He said what he believed to be the truth bluntly, and sometimes very roughly.

The first object of a Pope's "consideration" should be himself. He must remember what he is:

"Consider that you must be the model of piety, the champion of truth, the defender of the faith, the teacher of the nations, the leader of Christians, the regulator of the clergy, the shepherd of peoples, the avenger of crimes, the terror of the wicked, the glory of the just, the hammer that strikes down tyrants, the father of kings, the moderator of laws, the dispenser of canons, the salt of the earth, the light of the world, the priest of the Most High, the Vicar of Christ, the Anointed of the Lord."

No one can accuse Bernard of having diminished the dignity of the Holy See.

But then Bernard reminds the Pope of the humility of his origins. Facing the Pope's greatness, he places the nothingness from which this greatness emerged. The abyss between these two extremes is filled by virtue:

"Have faith, have piety, have wisdom, but the wisdom of the saints, which is the fear of the Lord.... Have prudence, justice, temperance. Above all, have humility, which is the most beautiful ornament of a Sovereign Pontiff."

The second object of a Pope's "consideration" is his house. How will he govern the Church, if he is not able to govern his own immediate entourage? Rigorous order should prevail in the management of affairs in the Pope's immediate circle.

But more important than the matter of housekeeping in the strict sense, is the coterie of churchmen around the Pope. Bernard made it one of the Pope's pressing duties to watch over all members of this staff of clergymen.

"It is not only unchasteness that must be banished from the papal palace, but everything that smells of laxity and worldliness. No children with long curls, no young men with curled hair around you, as are seen around certain bishops. It is not fitting that overly adorned heads should appear among the mitred heads."

The Pope must be a father, but also a leader and master. He must command respect by inspiring love. No silly jokes around him, no frivolity.

Then Bernard turned to the highest prelates of the Papal Court, the cardinals. At that time there were six cardinal-bishops, twenty-eight cardinal-priests, and eighteen cardinal-deacons. The entire Sacred College consisted of fifty-two cardinals. It was they who had the responsibility of dealing with all the great concerns of the Church. It was therefore necessary that the Pope choose his collaborators with utmost care and prudence. He should beware of glib speakers, of schemers, and ambitious men. Bernard pointed out:

"We in the cloisters accept all sorts of people, with a view to improving them. But it is not customary for the Curia to make clerics better. It is therefore easier and safer to accept clerics who are already good."

Bernard did not have equal regard for all the cardinals of his time. There were good cardinals, and some who were less so. It was in this work addressed to the Pope that he expressed his views most vigorously. Among those of the highest rank in the Church, he denounced "those who run after gold instead of running after Christ, who empty purses instead of reprimanding crimes, who enrich themselves and their families with the property of widows and the patrimony of the Crucified" (*De Consideratione*, IV, 4, 12).

Bernard wanted the Pope to follow Jesus' example and take up a whip to drive the money-changers out of the Temple.

After the cardinals, he dealt with the bishops. A Pope's authority and vigilance extends to all of them. But the Pope must remember that the Church is not "a piece of property to be exploited, but a function to be performed." The Pope is the sentinel of this world, he does not own it but is charged with guarding and preserving it.

Bernard insisted on this point: "I do not dread the sword or poison for you as much as the passion to dominate" (*ibid.*, III, 1, 1).

The Pope is responsible not only for his own actions, but for those of his representatives. He sends legates into every land to make decisions in his name. But he must choose these legates with the utmost care. Here again, it is the danger of cupidity that Bernard decried most forcefully:

"If they return to Rome exhausted, let it not be under the weight of their plunder. If they glorify themselves, let it not be for having amassed the most unusual and precious things in the lands they have visited, but for having brought peace to kingdoms, law to barbarians, tranquility to monasteries, order to churches, discipline to the clergy" (*ibid.*, IV, 4, 12).

And Bernard cited examples of abuses of this sort, as he has done in some of his letters as well. The same thing applied to the legates as to the cardinals of the Curia. They were not all evil men, but then, too, all of them were not equally good. Bernard went so far as to say: "For a legate to pass through the land of gold without bringing back any of it, is a virtue from another age!" (*ibid.*, IV, 5, 13)

We understand what Bernard means when he praises an excellent legate for "refusing all gifts." There were too many people eager to offer presents to legates, in order to win their good will and obtain favorable judgments from them. Before the most recent liturgical changes, Psalm 25, which says of flatterers: "their right hands are full of bribes" was said at Mass every day. Gifts were an ancient form of bribery. Bernard denounced it in a way that seems somewhat excessive today. He was visibly horrified by this practice, and even called it "the Italian sickness" or "the Roman evil." Frequent appeals to the Holy See had greatly enhanced this evil. All of the Church's concerns converged toward Rome. Bernard had been painfully disturbed by the babbling of the pleaders at the Roman Court and their swarms of lawyers. Bernard did not want the sanctuary of justice to become a "robbers' den" *(De Consideratione,* I, 10).

Bernard also spoke out against the excessive expenses involved in appeals to the Roman Court. He related that it was commonly said: "There are too many people in the Curia who are inclined to favor appellants and their appeals." Hunting for appeals had become a profitable business. It was claimed on all sides that at Rome "with money one is sure of winning one's case." It is quite possible that in Bernard's day, as in our own time when this is still said, this saying was pure calumny. Careful historians are of the opinion that Eugene III gave the example of the most perfect disinterestedness, and that his own aversion for wealth was universally recognized. Bernard has declared: "It was said of him that he valued money no more than a bit of straw." Sacks of coins brought from Germany had been pushed away from the threshold of the Curia.

Bernard commented: "This is a novelty. Since when has Rome refused gold? It is not believable that Romans should have given such advice." And yet it was true. Bernard could not deny that under the rule of Eugene III the greed and cupidity against which he was thundering had indeed been banished from the Curia. But he explained that to his mind not even a shadow of suspicion should hover over Rome.

As Bernard continued his treatise, he reviewed other matters that deserved a Pope's "consideration": the infidels, the Jews, heretics. For each of these categories, he set forth a whole program of action, in which we find all the ideas of the great "Gregorian Reform" upon which Bernard based his efforts.

To quote the historian Augustine Fliche: "It is in this that the *De Consideratione* is related to the decrees of 1074-1075 that restored clerical purity, and that is why this treatise is a most interesting effort to repair the Gregorian structure. The Cistercian monk did not hesitate to replace its somewhat worm-eaten framework. In proposing certain modifications to the Roman administration, he remained faithful to the basic idea of the Reform, namely, the moral regeneration of the clergy and of the laity" *(Histoire de L' Eglise,* Vol. 9, page 38).

VIII
BERNARD'S SPIRITUALITY

Overall View

It may seem superfluous to write about St. Bernard's spirituality, after all we have already said about his life, his example, and his activity as a reformer. And yet, at the risk of repetition, we want to give a general picture of his spirituality as well as its uniqueness.

Bernard, as we have said, was a "Doctor of the Church." But we also know he hated speculation for its own sake. In this respect, he was unlike St. Anselm, as well as the profound mystics of the School of St.-Victor in Paris, especially Hugo and Richard.

It has been said of Bernard's ideas that they were "ordinary." By this is meant that he invented nothing, made no innovations, produced no original ideas. He drew his doctrine from the Sacred Books, from the Latin Fathers, especially Augustine, Ambrose, and Jerome. He also knew the Lives of the Desert Fathers in a Latin translation by Rufinus. And yet he has exerted enormous influence not only during the Middle Ages, but also in succeeding generations up to our own time.

Bernard's influence is the effulgence of his holiness, of his vigorous mind, and of his deep conviction. As we have repeatedly pointed out, he was at once a contemplative and a man of action. Nothing of importance happened in his time in which he did not have a part. But the principal reason for his immense success stems from two things: first, the emotional appeal of his writings, and secondly, their practical application.

Bernard spoke to the heart. He was fiery, impetuous sometimes to excess, but never cold, monotonous, or apathetic. And at the same time, he urged to action. He did not limit himself to words. He wanted acts, resolutions, accomplishments. When he spoke of Jesus, Mary, and the saints, it was in accents that stirred the emotions and roused enthusiasm. Bernard's sensibility was as great as his austerity, which was very great indeed, and sometimes burst forth in the midst of his most sublime mystical elevations.

Sensibility

There is a famous page in Bernard's commentary on *The Song of Songs* that is often given as an example of his sensibility. It was the year 1138. Bernard had just lost one of his favorite brothers, Gerard, the one who had been the cellarer, or steward, of Clairvaux. He had attended him in his dying moments, and repressed his tears of sorrow when he buried him. But a few days later, right in the middle of one of his magnificent Sermons on *The Song of Songs*, the following words seemed to burst from him:

"How long shall I dissimulate and keep hidden within my breast the fire that is burning my poor entrails? Pent up this way, it courses more freely through my veins and tears me apart more doggedly. How can I be concerned with *The Song of Songs* amid such sorrow? The violence of my pain carries my thoughts elsewhere, and the Lord's indignation dries up my mind.

"The one who provided me the means of devoting myself to study in God has been taken from me. And so my courage fails me. Until now, I did myself violence, I controlled myself, so that my emotion might not appear to be stronger than my faith.

"You know that when everyone else was weeping, I followed the funeral cortege without shedding a tear. Still without shedding a tear, I remained standing by the grave until the end of the funeral. Wearing priestly vestments, I recited for him with my own lips the customary prayers. According to usage, I threw a little earth with my own hands on the body of my beloved who was about to become earth in his turn!

"People wept to see me, and there was surprise that I did not weep. It was not he, but myself who inspired pity, because of the loss I had just sustained. With all the strength of my faith, I repressed my innermost sentiments, striving with myself not to be shaken by the blows of nature.... But alas! although I was able to hold back my tears, I could not overcome my sorrow.

"I was troubled and remained silent, as Scripture says, but sorrow thus stifled has taken deep root and become the more violent in the measure that it was more firmly repressed. I admit myself vanquished, I must give vent to my suffering. I can certainly let it be seen to the eyes of my children!"

Bernard continued talking a long time in this vein. He described the man for whom he was weeping, he told his virtues, he expressed his admiration and love for him, and above all, he cried out his pain. He deplored the terrible separation that death had brought by taking his brother.

We have cited this passage throbbing with emotion because it best expresses the powerful affection of this exquisitely refined heart. His spirituality could not fail to bear the mark of his deep, vibrant, and sincere sensibility. Bernard knew how to accept God's will, but he was able to come much closer to his hearers and readers of his own and later times by the poignant accents in which he expressed his capacity to love.

For he spoke with the same emotion about the passion of Christ or Mary's tears at the foot of the cross.

In this respect, Bernard certainly belonged to the lineage of Augustine. The reason he has exerted such a power of attraction through the ages lies in this very warmth of soul.

Now, let us look in some detail at Bernard's spiritual doctrine. It begins with humility, and rises to love, and reminds everyone of the means of attaining holiness. Let us follow him closely, step by step.

Bernard and Humility

Like Augustine, Bernard saw humility as the very foundation of all perfection. To quote one of his Sermons: "Unless the spiritual edifice is built on the foundation of humility, it will most certainly collapse."

But Bernard was not content to introduce this doctrine in his Sermons on *The Song of Songs* or other subjects. He wrote a complete treatise on humility, in which he proposed to describe what he called the *Twelve Degrees of Humility.*

Actually, his treatise addressed to Godefroy, abbot of Fontenay, the second daughter house of Clairvaux, was entitled *Treatise on the Degrees of Humility.*

Strangely enough, Bernard spoke of humility, only by setting it up against pride. He seemed to have a better understanding of pride than humility. Now, pride, according to St. Augustine, is "the disordered love of our own excellence." Therefore, according to Bernard, humility must be "*scorn for our own excellence.*" But this scorn is the true knowledge of what we are, it is being honest with ourselves.

How could we not be humbled by the mere knowledge of what we are?

The soul, according to Bernard, sees itself burdened with sins, weighed down by the weight of its mortal body, plunged into the worries of this world, sullied by the mire of carnal passions, blind, deformed, infirm, or crippled, grappling with a thousand errors, exposed to a thousand dangers, the prey to a thousand fears, inclined to vice and incapable of virtue by its own efforts. How then can the soul hold its head high with pride?

Finally Bernard came to the definition of humility that has been cited so often through the centuries. Humility, he says, is "a virtue by which man, knowing himself exactly as he is, is vile in his own eyes" (*Treatise on the Degrees of Humility*, I, 2).

If we study this definition carefully, it is possible for us to translate the internal logic of St. Bernard's spirituality as follows:

There is no spirituality without a desire for perfection. Now, if we are pleased with ourselves, we cannot make any progress. In the spiritual life, when we do not progress, we go backward. Therefore, humility, which consists in having a low opinion of ourselves, in *constant dissatisfaction* with ourselves, is indispensable to spiritual progress.

Humility is not only the point of departure of the spiritual life. It is its constant source of strength, its inner motor. Bernard has expressed this thought in his *Treatise* in the following terms:

"Those whom truth, that is to say, humility, has taught to know themselves and hence rendered vile in their own eyes, necessarily find that everything they used to love has become bitter to them. For by looking at themselves squarely, they are obliged to see themselves as they really are, and this sight makes them blush with shame. And as soon as they are dissatisfied with their state, they yearn for a better state, which they realize they cannot attain by their own efforts.

"In their intense suffering, they are like stern judges who, out of love for the truth, hunger and thirst for justice. And they have no other consolation than to demand of themselves a very rigorous reparation for their past, to the point of scorning themselves, and firmly resolving to reform in the future. But they are well aware that they cannot succeed in doing it by their own strength.... Therefore, they turn from divine justice to implore divine mercy" (*Treatise on the Degrees of Humility*, V, 18).

So we see the path Bernard has outlined for us leads by an almost imperceptible ascent to the love of God.

Bernard and the Love of God

Bernard had a truly unique theory concerning the origin and development of man's love for God. He presented it many times, and above all in a letter he wrote to Guigo, prior of the Grande-Chartreuse, and to the other Carthusian monks. This letter, like many of his other letters, is a veritable treatise. We cite it now, to complement what we have already said in Chapter III of this book.

In his letter to Guigo, Bernard first made a distinction in the ways of serving God:

"There are various ways of giving glory to God. There are those who praise God because He is almighty. Others, because He is good to them. Finally, the third group, who praise Him simply because He is good in Himself and of Himself. The first category consists of servants who act only through fear. The second are the mercenaries who are lured only by gain. The third is the group of the children who act only from sentiments of honor and respect for their fathers."

Evidently, Bernard wanted everyone to be included in the last category. And so, he went on to describe the steps in the ascent of this love for God:

"It is therefore true that man loves himself first for his own sake, because, being carnal, he cannot enjoy anything beyond himself. But as he clearly sees he cannot subsist through his own power, he finally understands how much he needs God. So he begins to seek Him through faith and to love Him. And that is how he loves God in this second degree of love, that is to say, because God is useful to him, and not because God is lovable in Himself. But when, because of his need for God, he has begun to seek Him and come closer to Him, most often through reflection, reading, prayer, and obedience to His commands, there results a certain friendship through which, little by little, he comes to a more intimate knowledge of God's perfections.

"After that, he comes to delight in God, and having experienced 'how sweet is the Lord,' he rises to the third degree of love, which makes him love God no longer just for his own self-interest, but because of the excellence and greatness of the divine nature."

Bernard seems to be giving a brief sketch of man's spiritual growth in this passage. A child first relates everything to himself. Without realizing it, he loves himself, and loves other persons only in the measure that he receives good things from them.

However, in religious families, a child very early hears about God. He learns that God is all-powerful and that everything we have comes from Him. So he begins to love God because of the good things he has received from Him and expects to receive. There is considerable progress later on, when study, meditation, the reading of Scripture, give the soul a growing admiration for God, for His Being, His beauty, and His infinite love. It is then he can attain to this third degree of love: love of God because of His perfection.

But Bernard conceives of still another, a fourth degree of love.

Speaking of the third degree, he wrote:

"It is in this degree that we make a very long pause. And I do not know whether it is possible for anyone to arrive during his earthly life at the fourth degree in which *man loves himself only for the sake of God.* Those who have experienced it can witness to it. As for myself, I do not think it is possible in this world. But it will certainly be possible when the good and faithful servant enters into the joy of his Lord and is inebriated with the excessive delights that are enjoyed in the house of God."

As Bernard sees it, the fourth degree of love is distinctly superhuman, and seems reserved for the life of eternity. In the quarrel between Bossuet and Fénélon on pure love, Bernard would undoubtedly have sided with Bossuet.

Here is Bernard's description of the fourth degree of love:

"The soul then finds itself — that is to say, in the life to come — wonderfully forgetful of self, and as if totally dispossessed of self. And it plunges totally into God, so that it no longer has any ties except with God and becomes one spirit with Him. I believe the prophet held these sentiments when he said

(Psalm 71:16): 'I will treat of the mighty works of the Lord; O God, I will tell of your singular justice.'

"He certainly knew he would enter into these abysses of divine omnipotence and simultaneously be delivered from all his bodily weaknesses, so that, no longer obliged to think of the needs of his body, his whole spirit would be totally occupied in contemplating the justice of his lovable Lord."

Such was Bernard's conception of the genesis of divine love in us. We start out with the child's egoism, and rise by means of the great transports of contemplation up to the love of God, which is never perfectly pure on this earth, but will become so in the life to come.

Present-day theology would have an objection to this view. It would not be ready to admit that the first degree of love Bernard described is really love. Bernard did not make clear enough the incommensurable distance between carnal love of the natural order and the supernatural love born of grace in faith.

But Bernard spoke magnificently of love of God. His treatise *De diligendo Deo — On the Duty of Loving God* — contains passages where the great tenderness and what we have called sensibility of his heart bursts forth. For instance:

"I shall love You, Lord, my strength, my mainstay, my refuge and my liberator! You are everything desirable and lovable for me. My God, my helper, I shall love You because of Your kindnesses as much as I can, not as much as I should, but at least as much as is in my power. I shall be able to love You more when it pleases You to increase my love, but I shall never love You as much as You deserve" *(De dilig. Deo,* VI, 16).

The Love of Jesus Christ

One of the most important points to note in the spirituality of St. Bernard is the poignant attention he gives to the humanity of Jesus Christ.

There have been mystical writers who implied that in the highest degrees of spirituality the soul attains God directly in His divine nature, and no longer needs to pass through the humanity of Christ. For them, it is as if devotion to His humanity were something inferior, transitory, a sort of stepping-stone provided for beginners, but which the "perfect" no longer need to use. Bernard did not hold this view, nor indeed did St. Teresa of Avila or St. John of the Cross.

At the same time, Bernard admitted that love of Jesus Christ, insofar as it is a *sensible* or *affective* love is only a stage leading toward what he called *spiritual* love.

Here is a passage from his Sermon 20 on *The Song of Songs*, which clearly expresses his thought on the subject:

"Notice that our heart's love can be sensible when its object is the humanity of Christ. The things Christ did or taught during His earthly life touch the human heart in a special way. The faithful Christian, filled with this love, is easily moved to compunction by reason of all that Christ calls to his mind. He is most eager to hear about the life of Christ, he reads with greatest attention, thinks most often and meditates with greatest joy about the life of Christ....

"To the Christian at prayer appears the picture of the God-Man at His birth, or being nursed, or teaching, or dying, or rising again, or ascending into heaven. These memories of necessity make his soul cleave to the virtues or purify it of its vices, deliver it from lust and calm its passions. As for me, I think the great reason that impelled the invisible God to become visible in the flesh and to converse with men was to bring carnal men, who can love only in a carnal way, to the salutary love of His flesh and then to raise them up little by little to spiritual love."

In passages of this sort, we get a glimpse of a *mystical ladder.* We shall now try to describe this ladder as Bernard conceived it.

The Mystical Ladder

If we have understood what Bernard was saying about the mysteries of Christ's earthly life, then mystical love goes through several phases.

In the first phase, this love is still *sensible.* And Bernard calls it *"carnal"* — *carnalis.* In this beginning of love, we allow ourselves to be stirred emotionally by the sweetness, the beauty, the charm of Christ's mysteries. We see Christ in the manger of Bethlehem, we adore Him with the shepherds and magi, we gaze at Him in the arms of Mary His Mother, our mind follows all the episodes of His mortal life, and finally visualizes Him in His passion, His agony, His crucifixion, death, resurrection and ascension. To do this is to nurture healthful emotions, but these emotions remain on the surface of the soul. It is a beginning, but only a beginning. We must raise our sights higher.

As this first love becomes more perfect and deeper, it becomes *rational* or *intellectual,* Bernard says. This is the second stage. It consists in firmly believing the teachings of faith concerning Jesus Christ, the great mysteries that constitute the Christian religion: the Trinity, the Incarnation, the Redemption, the foundation of the Church, the institution of the sacraments, etc.

In this phase, we categorically reject all heresies and hold them in horror.

This *rational* or *intellectual* love does not abolish *sensible* or *affective* love. In fact, the latter holds a very important place in Bernard's spirituality. He loved to talk about Christ and the various episodes of His life and death. He knew that in order to attain to *rational* or *intellectual* love, and then rise to *spiritual* love, we must begin by giving *affective* love the nourishment it needs to grow and thrive.

Bernard admitted that at the start of his conversion it was sensible love that stirred him. Many years later, he sometimes accused himself of being more deeply moved by the remembrance of one of his dear ones than by the thought of God! But he knew that we must constantly strive toward spiritual love. He showed his monks the goal to be sought in his Sermons on *The Song of Songs.*

"Actually, although this devotion to the humanity of Christ is a gift and a great gift of the Holy Spirit, the love that inspires it is no less carnal—*carnalem tamen dixerim amorem*—in comparison with this other love that does not focus so much on the Word made flesh as on the Word-Wisdom, the Word-Justice, the Word-Truth, the Word-Holiness" (Sermon 20, 8 on *The Song of Songs).*

So Bernard was constantly striving with all his might to attain to this superior degree of love, without at any moment excluding love for the humanity of Jesus Christ.

As this is an important point in mystical theology, we shall develop it further.

Mystical Union

Bernard understood very well that it is through the humanity of Christ that we rise to His divinity:

"It is only in the very instant of mystical contemplation that the humanity of Christ is excluded. In other moments, mystics must carry out their duties to the humanity of Christ like everyone else. There is no mystical state in this life so lofty and so perfect that the humanity of Christ ceases to be the necessary means of reaching up to God."

In his Sermon 31 on *The Song of Songs*, he said:

"Take care not to think of anything corporeal or sensible in this union of the Word with the soul. We call to mind here what the Apostle says: 'Whoever is joined to the Lord becomes one spirit with him' (1 Cor. 6:17). We express as well as we can the ecstasy of the pure soul in God or the pious irruption of God in the soul. We use our poor words to express spiritual things in a spiritual language (1 Cor. 2:13).

"This union is effected in the spirit,...because God is Spirit and because He has become enamored of the beauty of the soul He has found walking according to the spirit, not yielding to the desires of the flesh and above all afire with divine love."

Commenting on *The Song of Songs*, in which the marriage of the soul with its God is described, Bernard could not fail to speak of this highest peak of union with God that is called "mystical marriage."

In his view, when the soul has become firmly established in *spiritual* love, it may be called by God – and Bernard insists on this point – to *"spiritual marriage."* He points out that the soul has now in some way reached the nubile age. It will therefore become *"the bride of the Word."* He expresses it this way:

"When the soul has reached this degree of love, it dares to think of spiritual marriage. And why would it not dare? It is all the more nubile in that it sees itself more like God. It is not frightened by the majesty of the Bridegroom....

"Therefore when you see a soul, having left all things, unite itself with all its might to the Word, live by the Word, follow His guidance, conceive by the Word what it is meant to bring forth for Him, a soul that can say: 'For, to me, life means Christ; hence dying is so much gain' (Phil. 1:21), know that this soul is the spouse of the Word and that it has contracted a spiritual marriage with Him" (Sermon 85, 12 on *The Song of Songs*).

This spiritual marriage presupposes a complete conformity of wills. Speaking of such a soul, Bernard said:

"If it loves perfectly, it is a spouse. What is sweeter than to experience this conformity of wills? What is more desirable than this love!... This contract of marriage is truly holy, truly spiritual. Contract is too weak a word, for it is an embrace — *complexus*. A veritable kiss in which the identification of wills makes of two spirits one and the same" (Sermon 83, 3 on *The Song of Songs*).

Ecstasy

Bernard then went on to describe the loftiest mystical states, speaking as one who had experienced them albeit only for fleeting moments.

He described those instants when all contact with the external world is suspended, when the soul is in God in a state of peace beyond expression, because "the tranquil God makes everything tranquil within the soul."

When this happens, the soul has truly penetrated into the holy of holies:

"In this secret place, within this sanctuary of God, if by chance one or another of you has been drawn into it and hidden within it for an hour, in such a way as not to be distracted by anything, or troubled by the needs of the senses or the goad of problems, or remorse of conscience, or — and this is more difficult — by the phantasms of sensible images, such a man, when he returns to us, can glorify himself

and say: 'The Lord has taken me into his chamber'"
(Sermon 23, 16 on *The Song of Songs;* see also
Sermon 45).

These are states beyond description. Bernard
speaks of them with admiration, but he says the
soul *"is unable to tell what it experiences at such
moments."* And yet, even if the spouse is as it were
asleep in this state, the soul is awake. It is ecstasy,
it is the sleep of the senses and the imagination. But
it is also the moment when the spouse receives the
greatest interior light and the most extensive knowledge of the Christian mysteries. This spiritual
activity reaches dizzy heights. And yet Bernard does
not claim these visions excel those which St. Paul
describes as seeing in a mirror, indistinctly (cf. 1 Cor.
13:12). It is not yet the beatific vision, for that is
reserved for eternity. Bernard assumes these are
spiritual images, produced in the soul by angels and
not originating in the subject's imagination. God does
not yet reveal Himself openly. Mystical contemplation, even in its most wonderful transports, remains
in the realm of faith. But it is on the threshold of
"vision."

Bernard also tells us that "this vision does not
terrify, but has a calming influence. It does not
over-excite the curiosity, but satisfies it. It does not
exhaust, but gives rest. It is truly quietude" (Sermon
23, 16 on *The Song of Songs).*

At such times, the whole soul sings! But it does
not sing an earthly song. Let us see once again how
Bernard expresses it:

"This song can only be learned by unction.
Only experience can give some idea of it. Those who
know the song, know the experience; those who
don't know the song are afire with yearning not so
much to know as to experience the unction. It is not

a word spoken by the mouth, but a song of the heart. It is not the sound of the lips but a surge of joy. It is the harmony of wills and not of voices. It cannot be heard outside, for it does not resound in public. Only the one who sings and the one to whom the song is sung, that is to say, the spouse and the Bridegroom, hear it. It is truly a nuptial song, expressing the chaste and sweet embraces of spirits, harmony of sentiments, and mutuality of desires" (Sermon 1, 11, on *The Song of Songs*).

Let us try to imagine what impact such words had on the monks who heard them. They must have been set on fire with love of God. And how they must have admired their teacher!

We must repeat, however, that for Bernard as for all the mystics, these were but brief and transitory moments. Moments when the soul touches God, so to speak, but only for a split second.

Bernard could not help saying: *"Alas! this hour comes rarely! and the instant is so short!" parva mora!*

"And after the Word has gone, the soul can only utter the same cry over and over, it has only one desire that it continually expresses, only one word it is forever repeating, until it happens again: *Revertere!* Come back!" (Sermon 74, 2, 3, 4 on *The Song of Songs*)

On another occasion Bernard exclaimed: *"If only it would last! Visit me again, Lord!"* (Sermon 23, 15)

There is so much joy in these brief moments. While they last, the soul is so far from temptations, from all the miseries of earthly life.

"For in its ecstasy, the soul, although it does not depart from life, at least departs from the life of the senses. Inevitably, therefore, it no longer feels temptation."

When Bernard speaks of these mystical experiences we have the impression he is not telling everything, that he feels a certain embarrassment about the graces he has received from God, and doesn't want his monks to get too high an opinion of him. He even seems as though afraid of being mistaken. He speaks with moderation and prudence:

"Who is wise enough to understand these things, to the point of being able to distinguish them properly from one another, and give a clear idea of them? If someone asked me that, I would decline to answer, preferring to hear them explained by someone who has experienced them, and for a long time. But such a person, whoever he may be, prefers, out of modesty and reserve, to hide what has happened within the depths of his soul and thinks it is safer to keep his secret to himself. Therefore, I who speak out of duty and cannot be silent, I tell you what I know from my own experience and from the experience of others, and what many can experience easily, leaving the loftier mystical states to those who are capable of understanding them."

Let us ask no more of Bernard than this. We shall close this chapter by citing a beautiful passage from his Sermon 79 on *The Song of Songs,* on love. His whole soul speaks through it.

"Oh! What a great thing is love! O divine love — impetuous, vehement, burning, divine love, who permit no thought but of Yourself, who despise everything else, who disregard everything providing You obtain what You want! You eliminate distances, You pay no heed to custom, You spurn moderation!

"Throughout this *Song,* it is love that speaks. If we want to understand what it says, we must love. It is useless to read or listen to love's song, if we do not love. A cold heart cannot understand words of fire, just as we cannot understand a discourse in Greek or Latin or any other language, if we are ignorant of Greek or Latin or any other language. Thus, for anyone who does not love, the language of love is a barbarous language.... Those who have received from the Holy Spirit the grace of loving understand this language and in answer to its words of love which they know very well they respond at once in the same language, that is, by works of love and piety!" (Sermon 79, 1 on *The Song of Songs*)

BERNARD'S
LAST YEARS AND DEATH

A Continuous Ascent

For Bernard, the very essence of life consisted in a striving for holiness. In a letter addressed to a conclave of abbots in Soissons which he could not attend, he spoke of the necessity of *"always going upward."*

"We do not have a permanent city here on earth and we do not yet possess the city to come, but we are searching for it. You must either ascend or descend, and if you stop you will infallibly fall. Certainly, that man is not good who does not want to be better, and the moment you no longer want to become more virtuous you cease being good."

This was one of Bernard of Clairvaux' firmest convictions, which he had originally drawn from St. Augustine. So, until he died he never stopped his upward climb. His great soul overcame the increasing weaknesses of his body. His health never good after he ruined it by his excessive austerities at the start of his religious life. The rigors of the Cistercian Rule, which he fervently observed, gave him no opportunity to restore it. The added burdens of the vast projects he shouldered for the honor and good of the Church further exhausted his fragile health.

True, when he was obliged to preach, even though he was drained of strength and almost at death's door, he would suddenly be transformed, regain all his energy, eloquence and apostolic zeal. Then he would fall back into his debility after the superhuman effort was over.

It has been estimated that Bernard spent about one third of his monastic life outside his cloister. And he was a monk for 42 years—from 1112 to 1153. We can thus calculate that he spent a total of 14 years on his various journeys throughout Christendom. However, during this time of travel and activity, he continued to lead a monk's life as much as he could. That leaves a period of 28 years when he diligently practiced all the exercises of the Cistercian community at Clairvaux.

But whether he was in his abbey or outside of it, his interior life was one of continual ascent.

In the evening of his life, he continued to work. He also suffered several bereavements. We shall speak only of the latter, because they reveal some of his greatest friendships.

The Death of Suger

Bernard's friendship with Suger, abbot of St.-Denis and high minister of the French kings, brought glory to both men.

Suger is one of the great historical figures of twelfth-century France. He was born in 1081 and was thus nine years older than Bernard. Born into a poor family, at an early age he entered the Benedictine abbey of St.-Denis, at the gates of Paris. His intelligence and wisdom quickly singled him out among his confreres. At first he became a kind of legal adviser for his monastery, and then in 1122 he was named abbot of St.-Denis.

As early as 1124, in a royal act, King Louis VI the Fat called him "his intimate and his faithful counselor." Soon afterward Suger began to play a preponderant part in the government of France. At first his concern for affairs of state seems to have overshadowed his monastic obligations. And Bernard's intervention in this matter was almost miraculous.

In writing about the duties of bishops and abbots, Bernard inveighed with apostolic frankness against the pomp and luxury of the great prelates of his time. He was alluding very clearly to the abbot of St.-Denis, when he told, tongue-in-cheek, how surprised the common people had been to see an abbot surrounded by a brilliant escort of more than sixty horses. And Bernard expressed the moans of the poor folk who were offended by having all this magnificence displayed before their misery.

Fortunately, Suger took the lesson to heart and profited by it. He had the good sense to admit that Bernard was right, that he should listen to him and cooperate in the reform movement he was championing. Most probably, even before Bernard expressed his criticism in words, Suger had already had some inner twinges of conscience, some secret regrets for the luxurious life he was leading. In any event, he did reform himself and his abbey with admirable vigor.

Suger became his critic's friend. He and Bernard exchanged many letters which have been preserved and witness to their mutual affection in a most edifying and moving way. The plans for the crusade brought them even closer. In fact, when the abbot of St.-Denis was near death in 1150, Bernard rushed to his bedside. Suger had become for Bernard the personification of the statesman who wants to remain and indeed succeeds in remaining a man of God. In referring to Suger in one of his letters to Pope Eugene III, Bernard praised him in these words:

"He is a man above reproach in temporal matters, as well as in things of the spirit. When he is with Caesar, one would take him for a member of the court of Rome. And when he is before God, for a member of the heavenly court" (Letter 309).

Suger's death inevitably was an occasion for national mourning, but no one mourned him more deeply than Bernard. Early in 1151, when all hope was lost for Suger's recovery, Bernard had written him a letter of exhortation saying:

"Man of God, do not tremble when you strip off this man who is of earth!... What do you have in common with these remains, you who are on your way to heaven?..."

Suger had sent word to Bernard: "If I could see your angelic face just once before I die, I would depart with a sense of greater security from this miserable world!"

These were the thoughts and messages between these two great-hearted men when death was about to separate them.

Suger died on January 13, 1151, at the age of 72. On his tomb, these simple words were inscribed: *Here Lies Abbot Suger.* There was no need to say anything else.

A year later, Bernard lost a protector and friend in the person of Thibaut, Count of Champagne, one of the great feudatories of the French crown.

Bernard now felt his own strength slipping, yet refused to give up any of his great undertakings.

The Death of Pope Eugene III

Another of our saint's best friends was Pope Eugene III. Many of Bernard's letters to him have

come down to us. When he learned of his election
to the papacy in 1145, he wrote him a deeply moving
letter. He expressed his wonder that the man whom
he had until then called his son had suddenly become his father. From then on, the bond of their
friendship grew continually stronger, despite a small
passing misunderstanding. During the year 1151,
Bernard said to Eugene III in a letter:

"Your child is sicker than ever. My life is seeping
away drop by drop. I am certainly not worthy of
entering into life immediately" (Letter 270).

The year 1152 was even worse for Bernard.
Everyone was expecting to hear of his death, especially at the French Court and at Rome. However, he
still had enough strength to respond to the call of
the archbishop of Trier, who was begging him to
intervene to stop the civil war in Lorraine. This was
Bernard's last great effort, and it left him exhausted.
He returned to Clairvaux, never to leave it again.
But it was the death of Eugene III that was the last
telling blow.

The pontificate of this favorite son of Bernard's
had been a great boon for the Church. Eugene III
had made excellent use of the lessons he had learned
in the monastery before he became Pope, as well
as those Bernard had addressed to him at his own
request in the famous work *De Consideratione.*

When the news of Eugene III's death, which
occurred on July 8, 1153, finally reached Clairvaux, Bernard was himself felled by illness. We have
no text of that period that refers to his sorrow, but
it must have been very deep. From then on, he
declined rapidly. His stomach refused all food.
When the abbot of Bonneval sent him a few delicacies, he wrote him the following lines:

"We received your charity with joy, but without pleasure. For what pleasure can there be for a man to whom everything is bitter? The only thing that would soothe me would be to eat nothing at all. I can no longer sleep, and thus my suffering has neither respite nor cessation. All this pain comes from the stomach.... What little food it deigns to accept, it digests with extreme difficulty; but the pain would be even worse if it fasted completely from all food. And if sometimes it accepts a little more than usual, then I am in paroxysms of pain. My feet and hands are swollen, like persons who have the dropsy" (Letter 310, written just a few days before his death).

But how did Bernard accept his cross? Another passage from the same letter gives the answer and shows that his ascent continued unabated. In fact, he was getting close to the top!

"In all this, as far as the interior man is concerned, I say this like a foolish man, the spirit is ready in an infirm flesh."

So Bernard's soul remained in control, as his body crumbled. His soul remained free, calm, serene. He continued to dictate, to console, to exhort. He continued to celebrate Mass as long as he was able to stand up.

Bernard's Death

He was growing weaker every day. Soon he wanted to think only of eternity. When the bishop of Langres came to see him about important Church affairs, he was surprised to find him less attentive than before, and told him so. Bernard replied:

"Do not be surprised. I no longer belong to this world!"

When Bernard's monks saw he was about to leave them, they clustered around him, lamenting that he was leaving them orphans. He answered their plaints with tears, telling them he was divided between his love for his children and his love for Christ which was pressing him to go and join Him. According to his first biographers, he closed his exhortations and what we might call his spiritual testament with these words:

"I have few good examples to bequeath to you, but there are three points I offer for you to imitate and that I remember having observed to the best of my power: I have always put less trust in my own views than in those of others. When others wounded me, I never sought to avenge myself against the one who hurt me. I have avoided as much as I could scandalizing anyone, and if scandal did occur, I made every effort to quiet it down."

On Wednesday, August 19th, or Thursday, August 20th, Bernard asked for and received extreme unction and holy viaticum. After that, he spoke to no one except to God. And it was on that same Thursday, around nine o'clock in the morning, that he peacefully gave up his soul to his Creator.

During the following days, vast crowds of monks and laymen, princes, lords, and poor peasants from the nearest villages and towns pressed around his mortal remains.

Already, everybody invoked him as a saint. People kissed his hands, touched pieces of cloth, coins, or any object available to his body to make relics of them. The hour of his funeral had to be hastened to put an end to the invasion of the monastery. Bernard was buried in the tunic he had received from the holy Irish bishop, Malachy.

As early as 1155, two years after Bernard's death, all the documents necessary for his official canonization by the Holy See were ready. However, circumstances delayed the publication of the papal bull by Alexander III until January 18, 1174.

We have already said that Bernard was proclaimed a Doctor of the Church in 1830. In his panegyric, Fénélon said of his writings, most of which we have cited in this book:

"Sweet and tender writings, drawn from and woven of the Holy Spirit, you are a precious monument with which he has enriched the Church. Nothing can wipe you away. And as the centuries unfold, instead of pushing you into obscurity, they will draw light from you. You live forever, and Bernard will also live in you."

Daughters of St. Paul

MASSACHUSETTS
50 St. Paul's Ave., Jamaica Plain, Boston, MA 02130; **617-522-8911.**
172 Tremont Street, Boston, MA 02111; **617-426-5464; 617-426-4230.**
NEW YORK
78 Fort Place, Staten Island, NY 10301; **718-447-5071; 718-447-5086.**
59 East 43rd Street, New York, NY 10017; **212-986-7580.**
625 East 187th Street, Bronx, NY 10458; **212-584-0440.**
525 Main Street, Buffalo, NY 14203; **716-847-6044.**
NEW JERSEY
Hudson Mall—Route 440 and Communipaw Ave.,
Jersey City, NJ 07304; **201-433-7740.**
CONNECTICUT
202 Fairfield Ave., Bridgeport, CT 06604; **203-335-9913.**
OHIO
2105 Ontario Street (at Prospect Ave.), Cleveland, OH 44115;
216-621-9427.
616 Walnut Street, Cincinnati, OH 45202; **513-421-5733; 513-721-5059.**
PENNSYLVANIA
1719 Chestnut Street, Philadelphia, PA 19103; **215-568-2638.**
VIRGINIA
1025 King Street, Alexandria, VA 22314; **703-683-1741; 703-549-3806.**
SOUTH CAROLINA
243 King Street, Charleston, SC 29401; **803-577-0175.**
FLORIDA
2700 Biscayne Blvd., Miami, FL 33137; **305-573-1618; 305-573-1624.**
LOUISIANA
4403 Veterans Memorial Blvd., Metairie, LA 70006; **504-887-7631;
504-887-0113.**
423 Main Street, Baton Rouge, LA 70802; **504-343-4057; 504-381-9485.**
MISSOURI
1001 Pine Street (at North 10th), St. Louis, MO 63101; **314-621-0346;
314-231-1034.**
ILLINOIS
172 North Michigan Ave., Chicago, IL 60601; **312-346-4228; 312-346-3240.**
TEXAS
114 Main Plaza, San Antonio, TX 78205; **512-224-8101; 512-224-0938.**
CALIFORNIA
1570 Fifth Ave. (at Cedar St.), San Diego, CA 92101; **619-232-1442.**
46 Geary Street, San Francisco, CA 94108; **415-781-5180.**
WASHINGTON
2301 Second Ave., Seattle, WA 98121; **206-441-3300;**
HAWAII
1143 Bishop Street, Honolulu, HI 96813; **808-521-2731.**
ALASKA
750 West 5th Ave., Anchorage, AK 99501; **907-272-8183.**

CANADA
3022 Dufferin Street, Toronto 395, Ontario, Canada.